WRITING AND PUBLISHING SHORT STORIES

by Rayne Hall

WRITING AND PUBLISHING SHORT STORIES
Professional Techniques for Fiction Authors

by Rayne Hall

Book cover by Erica Syverson and Jasmine Bailey

© 2022 Rayne Hall

September 2022 Edition

British English.

TABLE OF CONTENTS

INTRODUCTION

Do you want to entertain readers with short tales? Do you want to know how to construct a powerful story plot that grabs the readers' attention and won't let them go?

Step by step, this guide shows you how to

- Find ideas that make great fiction

- Build solid plot structures

- Craft great characters, compelling conflicts and sparkling dialogue

- Keep stories from growing too long

- Sell your stories for publication

I'll share insider tips, such as how to win writing contests and how to make sure your story catches an anthology editor's attention.

This book is structured as a self-study course with lectures, professional tips, hints about novice mistakes to avoid, and practical assignments which will guide you to write at least one complete story.

I use British English. If you're used to American English, some words, spellings, punctuation marks and grammar points may look different.

Now let's start your creative journey by choosing the stories you will write.

Rayne

CHAPTER 1

COLLECTING POWERFUL STORY IDEAS

In this chapter, I'll show you how to harvest ideas – the kind of ideas which make good story material.

The first trick is to collect all the ideas, and then to combine several of them into a story. One idea on its own is like a seed falling onto barren soil: it rarely germinates. It's when several seeds come together that the magic happens and the creative process begins.

The second trick; know what ideas to gather. Although anything can become a story, some ideas work better than others. The best ideas are the ones which have a personal connection with your conscious or subconscious mind. They will flourish the way they won't for anyone else.

I recommend that you start ideas lists – either in a pretty notebook or in a file on your computer. Populate them now with as many items as possible, and add to them continuously.

PLACES

Think of places you've been to which stirred your emotions (whether it felt creepy or safe), aroused your curiosity or have stayed in your memory for a long time. How about the house you grew up in, or the burnt-out ruin you used to walk past on your way to school, that luxury villa where nobody ever seems to be at home, the tree hut where you used to hide as a kid, your grandmother's cosy kitchen, the dank cellar, the stalactite cave where smugglers used to hide their contraband, the mysterious storage closet, the ancient castle you visited on your holidays, the forest hut where you once sheltered from a downpour, the beach hut, the creepy elevator, the five-star restaurant where you felt too intimidated to talk, the abandoned rollercoaster, the English high street at pub-closing time, the concert hall your mother tells you is haunted....

CHARACTERS

Whenever you get an idea for a person who could feature in a story, write it down. This doesn't need to be a fully fleshed-out character, it may be just a feature that intrigues you: the woman who spends all her spare time composing music to which no one ever listens, the firefighter who won a medal for his bravery and is a passionate cross-stitch embroiderer, the teenage boy who is convinced that he has a twin brother even though his mother denies this...

OCCUPATATIONS

Think of all the jobs you've held: not just your current employment, but the kind of work you started out, the freelancing you did on the side, flipping burgers or cleaning offices to finance your college studies, the side hustle you practised for a couple of years, the newspaper round or lawn-mowing gigs you did to earn pocket money as a kid, or helping your dad in his workshop.

All these have provided you with valuable insider knowledge which will give your stories authenticity. Include only work you've done yourself, not the glamorous occupations you've read and fantasised about.

HOBBIES

List any hobbies you are practising – or used to practise – with passion and skill. Can you perform magic tricks or build wooden furniture? Do you read the tarot, grow prize-winning giant onions, entertain your friends as an amateur stand-up comedian? Did you use to play the piano, create ceramic pottery, maintain a butterfly habitat in your back garden? In your youth, did you perform as part of a church choir, or a belly dance troupe, a figure-skating team?

These can provide vivid, believable backgrounds for short stories.

DREAMS AND AMBITIONS

Think of the dreams you had, pursued, fought for, gave up or still hold. Did you want to emigrate to a country on the other side of the globe, climb Mount Everest, become the first woman to swim across your region's lake, make it big in Hollywood, live in New York City, work as a photo model, manage your own company, become a theatre set designer, date a famous actress, win a medal in the Olympics, marry a millionaire?

These ambitions – how you felt about them, the steps you took to achieve you goals – can inspire a character's similar ambitions.

VALUES AND IDEALS

What are the values you hold dear? Do you believe in honesty, courage, loyalty or compassion? Does freedom or safety matter more than anything else? Perhaps your family or your faith is at the core of your life.

Do you admire people who always carry out what they commit to, or those who always treat everyone with absolute fairness?

Write down the values you feel strongest about. They can become a story's empowering theme.

DILEMMAS

Have you had to make tough choices in your life? Were you forced to choose between the career which meant everything to you, and caring for your mother in the final stages of her illness? Did you have to choose between two men whom you loved? Perhaps you had to give up your baby for adoption in order to continue going to school. Maybe you could have gone to college and fulfilled your dream of becoming a teacher, but decided against this because it would have deprived your ageing parents of their retirement fund?

Also think of the inner conflicts of other people. What difficult choices did your friends have to make? You can include dilemmas you've only heard about, even those you've seen in a movie or read in a novel. If a dilemma has stayed in your mind and engaged your thoughts, you can give it a fresh interpretation in a story.

PERSONAL FANTASIES

What scenarios engage your mind when you daydream? Do you fantasise about bravely coming to the rescue of a trapped family, about beautiful female feet in high-heeled sandals, or about living off the grid in a forest hut? As a kid, did you imagine yourself as a princess or a pirate queen?

Don't judge your fantasies. Just write them down. A keyword is enough.

TURNING POINTS IN YOUR LIFE

What events had a profound impact on you, changing your life's direction? Were you swept off your feet by a wonderful man and got married, even though you had planned to stay single? Did the spouse who had vowed to cherish you forever dump you in middle age? Did the person you trusted most betray you? Did a car accident rob you of your legs and mobility? Did you lose the job and income you had counted on? Did an inheritance suddenly make you rich? Did a prize in an art competition catapult you to fame?

Good or bad, these turning points yield intense fiction material.

MYSTERIES

Whenever something mystifies you, your mind is creatively engaged with the subject.

Why did your cousin really run away from home? Why does your father never talk about his first wife? Why did your aunt, who seemed happily married, suddenly divorce her husband? To whom did this brooch belong? Why is this woman selling an unworn wedding dress? Why is your boss taking a sabbatical? What is behind that wall? Where does this tunnel lead? Why is there a railway station in the middle of nowhere? What is this strange tool used for? Who used to live in your house?

Write down any puzzling objects, behaviours and situations you remember, and when you come across a fresh mystery, add it to the list.

ANYTHING ELSE

Whatever catches your attention or intrigues you is potential story fodder. Write the idea down before you forget it.

RANDOM COMBINATIONS

Some writers find that an element of randomness inspires their creativity. If you like the randomness, write each idea on a slip of paper, put them into a basket, and draw out five of them. Then try to combine them.

NOVICE MISTAKE TO AVOID

New writers are often attracted to 'random plot generators' – computer apps or printed cards which spew words and phrases which you then combine into a story.

Frankly, they rarely work, because the words and concepts won't resonate for you. Even if you manage to force a story around '*rowing boat + jealousy + fountain pen + kangaroo*', it will have no emotional power.

PROFESSIONAL TIP

Whenever you think, 'I want to write a story about...' (perhaps because a topic inspires you, or because of a writing contest with that theme) read through your ideas list, and select those which could form a connection with the topic.

ASSIGNMENT

Write the headings on different pages of your notebook, one per page. (You can open a computer file if you prefer, but most writers find that this kind of exercise works best when you write by hand.) Set a timer for twenty minutes. Now write down as many ideas as you can in this time.

You can add more ideas whenever they spring into your mind.

CHAPTER 2

ARTIST BRAIN AND EDITOR BRAIN: CREATIVE AND CRITICAL PROCESSES

When you write, it's as if there are two different personalities working in your head – an artist and an editor.

I call them Artist Brain and Editor Brain.

Artist Brain excels at creative challenges, problem solving, playfulness, coming up with ideas, freewriting, brainstorming, originality, first drafts, spontaneous plotting, creating new stories... all of which are crucial for writers.

Editor Brain is good for analytical thinking, critical assessments, structuring plots, revising, editing, finding and correcting errors, tightening, business matters, formatting … also crucial for writers.

Traditionally, it has been said that the left half of the human brain is analytical, and the right half creative. Although few modern scientists still subscribe to this model, you can use it to visualise the differences. Imagine Editor Brain living in the left half and Artist Brain in the right.

To create a great short story, we employ both – but at different times. Coming up with ideas and writing first drafts is a job for Artist Brain. Structuring the story and revising it is a job for Editor Brain.

Ideally, the two work together as colleagues, each doing what it's best at. In practice, the cooperation isn't always so smooth.

Editor Brain is often the assertive, jealous type, and sometimes it's a real bully. It can't bear to stand back and let Artist Brain get on with something. It interferes and censors, and tries to sabotage whatever Artist Brain does. It says things like, "This is crap." "This will never work." "This can't be done." "Hopeless." "Give up writing."

Artist Brain is the shy, sensitive type, easily intimidated, and freezes into inactivity when bullied. This can lead to a lack of creativity, dull prose, or writer's block.

Astonishingly, Artist Brain performs best under pressure and loves deadlines, the tighter, the better. That's why many writers find that timed writing challenges, contests with deadlines and writing marathons get their creative juices flowing. Given an impossibly tight deadline, you may produce your best-ever story.

Editor Brain, however, prefers time to carry out a job with slow, meticulous attention.

HOW TO ENCOURAGE YOUR ARTIST BRAIN

If your Artist Brain is cowering in the corner, here are four techniques for coaxing it into action:

- Use your non-dominant hand to do things for a few minutes (e.g. if you're right-handed, brush your teeth with your left hand). Many people find that this stimulates Artist Brain to become more active.

- Do some doodling, preferably in bright colours and in curvy lines. Artist Brain loves bright colours, circles, curves, and randomness. (Editor Brain prefers order, purpose, squares, straight lines, and black on white). Many writers find that a few minutes of doodling releases a pent-up creativity.

- Draw 'mind maps' using free associations, circles, curvy lines and coloured pens.

- Participate in short story writing contests with tight deadlines to give Artist Brain the chance to flourish under pressure.

This chapter, and the next one, are jobs for Artist Brain. Tell your Editor Brain to take a vacation so that Artist Brain can work undisturbed.

Editor Brain will have a starring role in some of the later chapters.

FUN WITH TITLES

For this assignment, you'll use Artist Brain. Artist Brain loves handwriting and colours, so you may want to do the exercise on paper with coloured pens. On the other hand, you may prefer to write it on your computer, since it saves typing it up afterwards. Maybe you can set your computer to use coloured fonts.

Get a kitchen timer or similar and set it for ten minutes.

During this time, write a list of title ideas. Just story titles, nothing else. Use your idea lists in Chapter 1 for inspiration, but don't feel restricted. If something comes to your mind, write it down, without censoring it. (Editor Brain may try to censor. Tell it to shut up.)

Ideas for story titles will probably come very fast. For example, if your list of settings includes modern day Shanghai, and the other lists include dragons, love and revenge, you can create titles like this:

Dragons

The Dragon

Dragons In Love

The Dragon's Revenge

The Third Dragon

Love of a Dragon

The Dragon's Lover

Vengeance

The Dragon's Egg

The Dragon's Nest

The Dragon's Mate

Three Dragons

To Love a Dragon

The Revenge

A Lover's Revenge

A Lover's Vengeance

The Vengeful Lover

The Dragon's Daughter

The Vengeful Dragon

Dragons in Shanghai

Vengeance in Shanghai

The Dragon of Shanghai

Shanghai Dragons

Shanghai Love

The Dragon's Daughter

My Daughter in Shanghai

My Mother's Vengeance

The Gambler of Shanghai

and so on.

Keep going for ten minutes. In this time, you'll get a long, long list.

You can continue another time, adding yet more titles. Indeed, you may find ideas for titles flowing into your head while you take a shower or wash the dishes.

NOVICE MISTAKE TO AVOID

Don't let Editor Brain interfere with Artist Brain's work. Editor Brain's critical, disapproving attitude can stifle your creativity, kill the fun or cause writer's block.

PROFESSIONAL TIP

Imagine Artist Brain and Editor Brain as separate creatures – your employees, or perhaps as team members. Treat both with respect, and set each to work on the areas they're best at. If one tries to interfere with the other's work, say firmly, "This is not your job. I have important work for you later." I find this helps a lot.

ASSIGNMENT

After compiling the titles, take a short break. Make yourself a cup of coffee, drink a healthy glass of water, pet your cat, do some stretches or light aerobic exercise. Now look at the list of titles with fresh eyes. Keeping your mind still in Artist Brain mode, highlight the titles which pique your interest, the ones which would get your attention and curiosity if you saw them in a short story anthology. Highlight them, preferably with a bright colour.

CHAPTER 3

THE PLOTLET CHALLENGE: A CREATIVE LEAP OF FAITH

When I tell you what I want you to do in this chapter, you'll probably squeal, "What?! That's impossible. It can't be done. Rayne is crazy!"

But that's just Editor Brain. Artist Brain loves this kind of challenge and will dance with excitement.

So tell Editor Brain to take the day off and let Artist Brain get to work.

I've used this practical assignment in many writing workshops from beginner to professional level, and every time, the writers gasped and squealed. But every time, they dug up gold. So trust me.

This is powerful stuff, almost supernatural in its effects. For it to work, you have to follow my instructions precisely, and you must suspend disbelief. And you must send Editor Brain away.

Squeal if you must, but do it anyway.

Here's what you will do:

You will create six stories out of nothing in just half an hour.

Yes, you read this correctly: six stories in half an hour.

Trust me: your Artist Brain is up to this crazy challenge.

The stories don't have to be detailed – maybe just two sentences long, with no characterisation, description or dialogue. They don't have to be good. Indeed they can be crappy, silly, pointless, daft... everything Editor Brain hates. Just do it.

Look at your list of titles – the ones you highlighted as interesting – and for one after the other, write a plotlet.

EXAMPLES

Since you may struggle with the concept of story plotlets (or just not believe it can be done), I've copied some of my own plotlets.

These are from several years ago when I set aside half an hour every day to write plotlets. Many were really bad, but some later grew into fine stories. As you can see, each plotlet is more or less a complete story.

The Angry Gardener

A woman who is passionate about gardening feels angry and helpless about the bullying neighbour who interferes with her gardening. She uses her anger as power for magic and turns him into a garden gnome.

The Chinese Doll

A couple are given a doll which is supposed to protect the wife during pregnancy. The wife finds the doll horrid and scary and can't bear the eyes. Although the superstitious husband wants to keep it, she destroys it. When the child is born, it has the same horrid eyes as the doll.

Love Spell

An intellectual woman is desperately in love with a man. He doesn't requite her feelings. She thinks he likes stupid women, so she trades her intelligence for beauty. But he still doesn't want her. Instead, he marries an intelligent intellectual.

The Painted Staircase

In an art gallery, a painting is so real that anyone who studies it intently gets sucked into the scene. It's a scene of a shipwreck. This happens to someone who then tries to get out. But he can't get out of the picture back into reality. Before he drowns, he realises he can get into another picture. He focuses on a picture of dry land. He gets pulled into that picture instead. But it's a picture of an ancient Roman arena in which he gets eaten by lions.

The Body In The Hearse

Driving behind a hearse with an open coffin, the driver sees the body move. He wonders what to do about this, and decides he must be mistaken and does nothing.

Demon Dancers

A dance troupe perform a folkloric demon dance when they realise there is one dancer too many among them. This upsets the choreography. Since they all wear masks, they can't identify the intruder. They cope as best they can. After the performance, the extra dancer vanishes. They realise that a real demon had joined the dance.

Are these plotlets great fiction? Of course not. But they're great starting points for wonderful stories. I've written these stories – and got them published.

Look at the first one, 'The Angry Gardener' – a title conceived from my interest in gardening, and my anger about a bully – which seems a rather daft plotlet, doesn't it? But it turned into a delightful story which was snapped up by the first market I sent it to, and has been published several more times since then.

Had I not allowed myself to write a 'daft' quick plotlet, this story would never have happened. I've included the stories resulting from 'The Angry Gardener' and 'Demon Dancers' at the end of this book, so you can read them. (The titles are now 'Gunda's Gnomes' and 'Thirteen Kukeri'.)

NOVICE MISTAKE TO AVOID

Of course, Editor Brain will tell you that this sort of thing is simply impossible. Don't listen.

PROFESSIONAL TIP

If Artist Brain is a little shy at first, help it by starting, 'Once upon a time there was a … [a dragon, a vampire, a single dad, a puppy, a whatever is mentioned in the title] who wanted/needed…'

Artist Brain loves 'Once upon a time there was…' openings.

ASSIGNMENT

Get a kitchen timer or other timing device, and your list of titles. Set the alarm to five minutes. Pick one of the underlined titles, and write. You have five minutes to write a story.

If possible, invent stories that take place inside a short time span, perhaps an hour or a day.

Don't try to write a good story. Just write a story. Don't let Editor Brain near it. Keep an eye on the time. You don't have time for details. When the alarm beeps after five minutes, pick another underlined title and start the next story.

When the thirty minutes are over, stop writing. Take a deep breath, make a cup of tea, and relax. You're probably convinced that what you've written is rubbish, and that none of these plotlets can be made into anything resembling a decent story.

But you'll be surprised – because Artist Brain is fantastically creative, especially under time pressure, as long as Editor Brain isn't watching.

Once you've had your cup of tea, tidy the mini stories up a bit, just to make them legible. Don't let Editor Brain near them yet.

If you belong to a writers' group, ask the members which of these six stories they find most intriguing. The result may surprise you. (Don't ask Editor Brain! Editor Brain would tell you that all six are crap.)

CHAPTER 4

FREEWRITING: JUST LET IT FLOW

In this chapter, Artist Brain is in charge once more. However, near the end of the chapter, there'll be a small job for Editor Brain.

Set your timer to twenty minutes. This is an Artist Brain activity, so keep Editor Brain out of the way.

Pick one of the plotlets you've written – the one you feel inspired to write right now, or simply the first one on the list.

For twenty minutes, just write. Let the ink flow from your pen, or the fingers dance across your keyboard. Don't stop to think, don't go back to correct. Just write as much as you can. Write anything which comes to your mind about this story: characterisation notes, description of a setting, ideas on how to create tension, questions, what-if scenarios, anything.

Don't pause. If you run out of ideas, just write the story's title over and over until ideas flow again.

This process is called 'freewriting', or if you like fancy terms, 'stream-of-consciousness writing'.

After twenty minutes, you may stop and take a break. If you're in full creative flow and wish to continue, you may keep going for longer.

When you've completed this task, take a break, maybe drink a glass of water and do some stretches. Then invite Editor Brain back in.

The next task is perfect for Editor Brain, who loves analysing things. Read what you've written, and underline anything that you feel would work well for your story.

NOVICE MISTAKE TO AVOID

Inexperienced writers often block their creative flow by editing when they should just go along with their ideas.

PROFESSIONAL TIP

You can use the freewriting method not just to develop ideas for the plot, but also later, whenever you feel stuck. For example, Mary and John are divorced – but for a certain scene to work, the two have to renovate a house together, an unlikely situation. Write the question 'Why are Mary and John renovating a house together now?' on top of the page, and do a twenty-minute freewrite. Your subconscious will come up with solutions.

ASSIGNMENT

Carry out the exercise I've outlined above: a twenty-minute freewrite about a plotlet.

CHAPTER 5

FROM IDEA TO PLOT

How often have you thought, 'I want to write a story about this' – and then waited in vain for the muse to come? You may have visited an intriguing place, listened to a friend's heart-wrenching marital woes, chuckled about a social media post, or heard about an astonishing true-life event. These ideas are like sparks, hot, bright and fascinating – but how do you get from idea to story, from a mere spark to a bright flame?

Staring at the spark, waiting for the muse to come and fan it into a fire, rarely works. The sparks die, and all that's left is a cold crumb of ember. To build a fire, you need tinder (crumpled newspaper, birch bark, cotton wool balls) which ignites when touched by a spark. Without tinder, you won't get a flame, and without a flame, you can't light the kindling which sets the logs on fire.

In this article, I'm going to give you the tinder that will grow your idea into a brightly burning flame.

Look at the ideas you've come up with during the freewriting assignment in the previous chapter, as well as the ideas list you've compiled earlier, as well as concepts which have been haunting your head for a while, demanding to be written. Pick one of them.

Here are five kinds of ideas. To which group does yours belong? Play with the questions, try out different answers, and before long, you'll have the basics of a short story plot.

1. THE 'PLACE' IDEA

You're visiting an interesting location – a historical building, a tourist attraction, a friend's home, a wild landscape, a quaint village, a danger site, a spectacular view – and your heart hammers with excitement because you know this could be the setting for a great story.

This is how most of my Gothic stories start: I explore remote, creepy, spooky places – ancient ruins, derelict factories, abandoned homes – and then put characters into them.

Questions to ask:

What kind of person might come to this kind of place? Why? What do they want here? Are they here voluntarily or against their will? Is someone with them, and if yes, who? Are they here to meet someone, and if yes, whom and what for? Are they trying to avoid someone, and if yes, whom and why? What if they don't realise that someone is already in this place? Who and why? What if someone arrives unexpectedly? Who and why? In what way does the new arrival cause a problem? How does the weather affect what they feel, what they need, what they do? How might the weather get worse, and what will they do about it? What can they do here that they cannot do in another place? What dangers might a character face in this place? What can they do to keep safe against those dangers? What do they not know about this place and find out later?

2. THE 'CHARACTER' IDEA

You observe someone's behaviour, hear their life story, listen to a friend telling you about someone they met, or get exasperated by a person's attitude. Or perhaps a minor character in a novel intrigues you, and you think, "I want to write a story about someone like her."

Questions to ask:

What intrigues you personally about this character? Why is this aspect so interesting to you? What is this main personality trait – can you define it in a single word? What shaped this person to become like this – perhaps their upbringing, their religion, a traumatic event? What kind of situations trigger the character to show this sort of behaviour? What are the two sides of the coin of the main character trait? Most traits have a positive and a negative side, for example, 'thrifty' and 'devout' are positive while 'stingy' and 'bigot' are negative, and this works really well in short stories. What benefits does the person get from their trait? What problems does it cause for them? What other people could benefit from the character's trait/weakness/flaw? In what way? Do they deliberately goad the character into this behaviour to take advantage? Who suffers as a result of the person's trait/behaviour/attitude? Are they trying to change the person? If yes, how, and with what results? What would have to happen for the character to change, learn or grow? What are the character's deeply held values? How do those values connect to the important trait or flaw? What's this character's self-image (how they see themselves)? Do other people see them the same way, or differently? How? What does this character want most? Why? What does this character need? Do they know they need it?

3. THE 'SITUATION' IDEA

While reading a book or watching a film, or perhaps hearing people talk about their life experiences, a certain situation captivates you. Examples: a woman suspects that her husband is a bigamist. A mature woman goes on a blind date arranged by her daughter. Five people jointly inherit a house but can't agree what to do with it. A man buys a retirement home and settles in, and then someone else claims to be the legal owner and proves it. Siblings meet again for the first time in fifty years. You know this situation deserves a story of its own, and your heart beats fast with excitement at the prospect of writing it.

Questions to ask:

What exactly is it that fascinates you about this situation? Why does it resonate so strongly with you? Does it bring up old memories, cherished daydreams, long-held romantic fantasies? To what kind of person could this happen, i.e. who might find themselves in such a situation? How did they get into this situation? How do they feel about it? What could they do about it? What will they do? (Tip: if you were inspired by someone else's story, make the main character, the preceding events and the resulting actions different. Don't clone the existing tale: create your own original story.) What dilemma does this situation pose (inner conflict)? Whom else does this situation affect?

4. THE 'INNER CONFLICT' IDEA

Someone tells you about a dilemma they face, or you hear about someone who was forced to make a horrible choice, or perhaps you yourself have to make a tough decision. A character forced to choose between her lover and her child, between love and loyalty, between their faith and their family, can kindle stories with great emotional power.

Questions to ask:

What kind of person (other than the one to whom it happened in reality) might face this kind of choice? How might they have gotten into this situation? What options do they have? In what way is each of these choices wrong? What are the disastrous consequences of each choice? Can you raise the stakes and make the consequences even more dire? Which of their personal values or beliefs are affected by this? With each option, what sacrifices would the character have to make? What other people might be affected by the character's choice? What do they have to gain or lose? Will they try to apply pressure on the character?

5. THE 'ACTIVITY' IDEA

While working in your day job or enjoying your hobby, you think, "I'd like to write a story about this." Or perhaps it's your friend's or brother's career that inspires you, or you watch someone carry out an activity or remember a task you used to do. Activities make great short story backgrounds, especially if you can write about them with authenticity of personal experience.

Questions to ask: what kind of person might practise this activity? (Tip: make your story interesting by avoiding stereotypes. How about a female boxer, a highly educated bodybuilder and a mature pop singer?) What are the routine tasks involved in this activity? What could go wrong while doing this? What are the risks and dangerous involved? (With knitting, the risks may be moderate – stitches may drop, or the cardigan may not be the right size for the child. With mountaineering, an incorrectly tied knot can be lethal.) Who or what can cause problems? For example, an inexperienced new team member may make a mistake, a business rival may sabotage the equipment, a careless colleague may skip safety measures. What might happen to disrupt a normal daily activity? What does a practitioner of this hobby/sport/profession dream of achieving? Could this be the goal they pursue during the story? Why is this so difficult to attain?

LIGHTING THE FIRE

I find that the best method for this is to write my answers by hand into a notebook, and to continue 'freewriting' the thoughts that come into my head, with Artist Brain in charge. Soon, the idea will ignite into a strong flame. You may even get several ideas. In this case, choose the one that excites you most. You can always return to the other ideas later and create more stories.

When you build a fire, you touch the spark (from the match, firelighter, flint etc.) to the tinder (bark, paper, cardboard, cotton wool etc.) to create a flame.

Your idea is the spark, my questions are the tinder, and your answers are the kindling. Together, they make the beginnings of a bright fire.

Now it's time to add the fuel (logs, charcoal, eco-briquettes etc.) to create beautiful, long-lasting heat. You can either develop a structured plot outline or write a first draft from the seat of your pants.

NOVICE MISTAKE TO AVOID

Inexperienced writers often forget to ask 'Why' questions at this stage.

PROFESSIONAL TIP

The most fertile question is 'What if…?'

ASSIGNMENT

Pick one of your story ideas. (It doesn't matter which one you take first. You can tackle the others later.)

Identify what kind of idea group it belongs to (e.g. is it a situation idea or a character idea), and ask the questions. Write down the answers, perhaps as part of another freewriting session.

CHAPTER 6

CHARACTER: WHO IS YOUR STORY'S BIG STAR?

In this chapter Artist Brain and Editor Brain work together.

Take the story you started working on in the previous chapters, and answer the questions below. (I use the female pronoun; you can of course choose to write about a male.)

1. Who is the character who needs or wants something? Choose her as the point-of-view character. If you're not familiar with the concept of point-of-view, here's a simple explanation: The PoV is the character through whom the reader experiences the story. Most short stories have only one PoV. The deeper you immerse your reader in the PoV, the greater the emotional power of your story.

2. What does the PoV want? Choose something that's achievable in a short time, perhaps inside a day, or better still, inside an hour. This keeps the story short. The shorter the timespan, the easier and quicker it is to write the story.

3. Why does she want it? Give her at least three reasons.

4. What is at stake if she doesn't achieve it? Think of at least one devastating consequence. You may choose more than one.

5. Optional: why does she need to achieve this by a certain time? Not all stories have this element, but if it suits your story, I recommend using it, because it increases the tension and suspense.

6. Describe this character's personality in three adjectives. Examples: 'kind, musical, greedy', 'curious, intelligent, arrogant',

'brave, honest, ambitious', 'loyal, creative, narrow-minded', 'pious, patient, vain'.

Artist Brain is good at inventing characters while Editor Brain is good at distilling the personality into three adjectives.

7. What obstacles might possibly stand between the character and her goal? List at least three ideas. Artist Brain is good at supplying ideas for obstacles.

8. Who are the other characters in this story? Try to limit your story to between three characters (for a very short story) and seven (for a longer tale). This keeps the story short, and makes it easy to read.

If Artist Brain whines about cutting characters, let Editor Brain do it. Editor Brain is ruthless.

NOVICE MISTAKE TO AVOID

New writers often start by creating elaborate profiles, laying out every detail from the character's breakfast habits to her fashion sense. Then, when they start writing, they discover that the character they've invented doesn't fit organically into the story and doesn't act the way the plot requires.

PROFESSIONAL TIP

Develop the main character and the plot organically side by side. Decide early on what kind of person could fulfil the role, but keep this basic, e.g. 'a nervous, musical young woman'. Once you've written the first draft, you'll have a clearer idea what kind of person she is, and that's the time to develop a fully-fleshed out profile. When writing the second draft, you'll know her well, and she will behave the way the plot requires.

With each layer of revision, you can refine the character as well as the plot.

I recommend developing the other characters as you go along. While writing the first draft, you'll discover what kind of characters are needed to tell the story. Some of them may surprise you by simply turning up uninvited. That's usually a good sign.

ASSIGNMENT

At this stage, you've spent some time with the emerging story, and will have a pretty good idea of the kind of person needed to fill the starring role.

Write down what you know about her so far, but remain flexible. As the story develops, the character may respond to the plot by revealing surprising personality traits.

CHAPTER 7

SIMPLE STRUCTURING WITH PLOT EVENTS

For this chapter, put Editor Brain in charge. Editor Brain will complete the job with minimal fuss in a short time.

To create a plot quickly, use the following blueprint for the structure. Editor Brain loves working with blueprints, even if Artist Brain sniffs at them.

The BASIC STRUCTURE

1. Beginning (includes Story Question)

2. First Plot Event

3. Second Plot Event

4. Third Plot Event (often includes a dilemma, danger or sacrifice – or all three)

5. Resolution

The *Beginning* is a situation which immediately kicks off the story. Typically it goes like this: 'When a situation arises, the character realises she needs to achieve the goal'.

From this situation arises the *Story Question*: 'Will (or: How will) the character achieve the goal?' Find a way to state the Story Question clearly. The more clearly you state it, the more the reader will care. The end of the first paragraph is often a good place for stating the Story Question.

Plot Event means something is happening.

'She feels lonely' is not an event.

'Feeling lonely, she agrees to go a blind date' is an event.

'He is close to giving up' is not an event.

'He is close to giving up when his sister comes to his aid' is an event.

The best kind of plot event is often this: 'An obstacle arises, and the character takes action to overcome it'.

A story may have more plot events, but be careful or your story will grow too long. If you get carried away, you may end up with a novella or even another novel. I recommend three to twelve plot events, depending on the length you're aiming for.

The *Resolution* answers the question of whether or not the character has achieved the goal. For example: yes, she achieves it, and lives happily ever after. Yes, she achieves it, but at a terrible price. Yes, she achieves it, but realises too late it was a mistake. No, she doesn't achieve it, but gains something even better instead.

In the next chapter, we'll delve deeper into goal, motivation, story question and resolution.

NOVICE MISTAKE TO AVOID

New writers often include too many plot events (which makes the story overlong and unwieldy) or non-events (which aren't important enough to be developed as plot events, and can make the story dull and dragging).

PROFESSIONAL TIP

Three or four plot events is good if you want to write flash fiction (very short tales). Five works well for stories of around 2,000 words. Twelve plot events are appropriate if you want your story to be around 7,000 words long.

Please note – this is just a broad guideline, your own stories may differ.

ASSIGNMENT

Go ahead and write the structure of your story. Write a one-sentence summary for Beginning, a one-sentence summary for each Plot Event, and a one-sentence summary for the Conclusion.

Don't write the story yet. Please beware: Artist Brain may try to interfere and tempt you to include lovely details. Stay firm, and keep Artist Brain away from this assignment. For now, Editor Brain is in charge and will produce a quick, concise structure.

CHAPTER 8

GOAL AND MOTIVATION: WHAT DOES YOUR STORY CHARACTER WANT, AND WHY?

In this chapter, I want to share a professional trick for hooking readers from the start and keeping them hooked until your story's ending.

Give your main character a goal and an urgent reason to pursue it. Perhaps she wants to win a prize in the village flower show, rescue her daughter from the kidnappers, get her suitor to propose marriage or raise money for her business.

Make this as important as possible: she doesn't just want it, she needs it. Give her a compelling reason (or better, several) for needing to achieve this.

Example: Mary needs to win a prize in the flower show to gain recognition from the villagers and to outdo her arch-rival Mrs Jones for once. The win will prove her gardening skill and make her an eligible candidate for president of the village horticultural society, a position she covets.

For other kinds of stories, the goals may be more dramatic: She needs to rescue her daughter from the kidnappers, because these men are violent and the police aren't taking action. She needs to get her suitor to propose marriage, because he's the only eligible bachelor in town, and she'll soon be an old maid. She needs to raise money for her business, because otherwise she'll lose her life's work and hundreds of employees will lose their jobs.

Raise the stakes. Think of ways to make the goal even more important. What would be the dire consequences of failing?

The more the character needs something, the more the readers will root for her to succeed. This will keep them reading, needing to find out if and how she gets what she wants.

This goal needs to be very clear — to you, to the character herself, and to the reader. So, state it at the beginning of the story, preferably in the first few sentences. Spell it out. Don't just imply it and hope that the reader will get the subtle hints.

REPEAT THE GOAL SEVERAL TIMES

Use different ways to state the goal several times during the story and keep it in the reader's mind. For example, by simply stating it. (For example, you might write near the beginning: *She had to win the prize for best floribunda rose.* A few paragraphs later, you could write: *This year, she would beat Mrs Jones to the trophy.*)

Dialogue is a good way. (*"Dinner is ready, honey." "I can't come now. There are aphids on a rosebud! If they spread, how am I going to win the prize for Best Rose?"*)

You can also use the character's thoughts. (*Mary held the bloom against the light, examining the pale pink petals for blemishes. 'Perfect. This is the one I'll enter in the contest,' she decided. 'Mrs Jones shan't have the trophy this year.'*)

Readers stay on the edge of their seats, needing to find out whether (and how) the character achieves her goal.

Make it difficult for her by putting obstacles in her way. Mary's roses get attacked by aphids, her ignorant husband cuts the best blooms to take a bouquet to his mother, and rival Mrs Jones' flowers look sensational.

ANSWER THE STORY QUESTION AT THE END

End the story by showing clearly whether the character has attained her goal. Did Mary win a prize in the village flower show?

If you don't answer this question, readers will feel unsatisfied with the story.

The answer can be 'yes': Yes, Mary won. Despite all obstacles, her floribunda rose earned the first prize. This gives your story a straightforward happy ending.

The answer can be 'no': No, Mary didn't win. Despite all Mary's efforts, her arch-rival Mrs Jones got the trophy again. This is a straightforward unhappy ending.

To make your story meaningful and memorable, avoid straight 'yes' or 'no' endings. Instead, close your story with a 'yes, but...' or 'no, but...' conclusion:

Yes, Mary won the prize – but her arch-rival Mrs Jones became horticultural society president.

Yes, Mary won the prize – but her obsession drove her husband away.

No, Mary didn't win the prize – but she was elected horticultural society president anyway.

No, Mary didn't win the prize – but she and her arch-rival Mrs Jones became close friends.

NOVICE MISTAKE TO AVOID

Many stories by inexperienced writers lack a story goal altogether, or don't spell it out soon enough.

PROFESSIONAL TIP

Shoot for 'yes, but' and 'no, but' endings, because these leave the greatest impact.

ASSIGNMENT

What does your story's main character want, and why?

Does she achieve it in the end?

CHAPTER 9

CONFLICT AND THEME: GIVE YOUR STORY MEANING

Do you want your story to be meaningful and memorable? Then give it a theme.

Although there are many ways of creating and exploring a theme, here's the one I find the easiest as well as the most powerful.

'One Purpose/Ideal/Value' versus 'Another Purpose/Ideal/Value'.

For example:

- Love versus Safety

- Patriotism versus Friendship

- Faith versus Integrity

- Honesty versus Compassion

Have a look at the recurring motifs you've identified for your writing; they sometimes contain purposes, ideals or values. Also look at the three adjectives with which you've described your main character, because they often contain purposes, ideals or values.

For example, if you've described your character as 'musical, ambitious and loyal', then 'Ambition versus Loyalty' makes a powerful theme, as well as intense inner conflict for that character.

This type of theme gives your story meaning and depth. It is especially useful if you've described the flavour of your writing as deep, meaningful, thoughtful, inspiring, serious, moral, thought-provoking, literary, heart-wrenching, emotional, character-led, or intelligent.

It will keep the reader thinking long after they've finished reading the story. The reader will consider how she would have decided and acted, and compare it with how the character responded.

A story doesn't need to explore a deep theme, and the theme doesn't need to be of the 'one purpose/value/ideal versus another' type. But it works wonders. Try it.

Your main character is torn between these two values. By adhering to one, she is betraying the other. This inner conflict can lead to heart-wrenching dilemmas.

Try to explore the theme in the outer conflict, too. A good way of achieving this is by using two characters who are both close to the PoV, with each representing one of the values, and the PoV is caught between them.

AN ALTERNATIVE WAY TO CREATE A THEME

Some writers like to weave a story around a proverb or saying, e.g. 'Love conquers all' or 'A bird in the hand is worth two in the bush.' You may want to try this approach one day and see if it inspires you.

Personally, I prefer a theme based on the dilemma of two important values, because this provides the story with an instant, powerful inner conflict.

NOVICE MISTAKE TO AVOID

Resist the urge to get preachy about the subject and to over-explain the meaning.

PROFESSIONAL TIP

Long stories may have a subplot that explores the same conflict from a different angle.

ASSIGNMENT

Let Editor Brain choose a theme which suits your story and your character. If Editor Brain comes up with several options, choose the one which moves you most.

Find several ways how your story can explore facets of this theme in inner and outer conflicts. Artist Brain will be good at coming up with ideas. Jot them down briefly; no need to explain them in detail.

CHAPTER 10

THE FIRST DRAFT: IT'S MEANT TO SUCK

The time has come to write the first draft.

Please note: this is a first *draft*. Write it quickly. Don't go back over your paragraphs, don't refine your sentences, don't deliberate over the perfect word.

Later, you'll make substantial changes to that first draft, so any fine polishing you do now would be wasted.

This is definitely a job for Artist Brain. Artist Brain is uninhibited and comes up with great creative work under pressure.

Don't let Editor Brain near your first drafts. Editor Brain would criticise, censor and sabotage every sentence you write. Tell Editor Brain to wait, its turn will come again soon.

If you find it difficult to let go of high expectations for the first draft, try walking around the room or the garden, repeating this sentence like a mantra: "First drafts are meant to suck."

Do you like baking? If yes, think of this analogy: the first draft is like assembling the ingredients for a cake, laying them all out on the table. The measuring, kneading and baking come later, and you need to have the ingredients before you can do any of those.

NOVICE MISTAKE TO AVOID

Novices usually try to write something good straight away, and feel frustrated when the result doesn't come up to their high expectations.

PROFESSIONAL TIP

I've come to enjoy the freedom of writing crappy first drafts – and I never let anyone read them.

ASSIGNMENT

Keep your exercises and notes from the previous chapters at hand, because you'll need them.

Decide how much time you want to spend on the first rough draft. I suggest one hour, perhaps two, but no more. As you've already experienced, Artist Brain is amazingly creative and productive when the time is limited.

If you allow more time, Editor Brain will take over, insist on getting everything 'right' and 'perfect', constantly revising and editing, so you'll barely get past the beginning. Your job is to *complete* the draft. It may be rough, it may be crappy – but it must be complete.

Set your timer.

Now write the story and take pride in its raw awfulness.

In the next chapter, we'll start improving on it.

CHAPTER 11

HOW TO KEEP YOUR SHORT STORY SHORT

Shorter stories are quicker to write. This means, you can produce more stories, and multiply your chances of getting them accepted for publication. But stories often expand as we write them, trying to grow into novels, demanding more and more words. How can you keep your short story short?

Here are six techniques that professional short story authors use. Apply them when you start plotting your yarn.

1. CONDENSE THE TIME FRAME

Let the action play out in the shortest time possible; a weekend, an afternoon, perhaps even just an hour. Plots spreading over weeks, months or years tend to grow into novels. Curb this by making everything happen quickly.

2. REDUCE THE CAST

Recruit only as many characters as the story needs. The fewer characters, the easier it is to keep a story short, so don't involve a cast of thirty when you can tell the story with three.

Combine several roles: the old school friend is also the piano teacher, the neighbour and the one who finds the treasure in the attic. This will not only keep the word count low, but give the story fabric a richer texture.

3. STAY IN ONE PLACE

Can the whole story play out in a single location? Then keep it there. This will make the story much shorter than if you set one scene in Istanbul, one in Copenhagen and the third in Rome.

If changing locations are crucial to the plot, use as few as possible. Let all Istanbul scenes play out in the Grand Bazaar, instead of hopping from the Bazaar to the Bosporus.

4. LIMIT THE NUMBER OF SCENES

The fewer scenes, the shorter the story. Write a list of the scenes you think you need, then see which of them can be combined. Could the scene where Mary finds the body also be the one in which she rejects John's proposal of marriage? Combining scenes will not only tighten the story, but give it a faster pace and make it more exciting to read.

5. LEAVE OUT CHUNKS WHERE NOTHING HAPPENS

Novice writers often pen passages which contribute little to the plot. Leave those out. Instead of describing the train journey from Copenhagen to the Istanbul, with descriptions of the bunk where she sleeps, the food she eats and the landscapes she sees on the way, simply write, "The train arrived in Istanbul at dusk."

6. SKIP FLASHBACKS

Flashbacks – sections where the main character relives past events – add heavily to the word count. They also disrupt the flow of the action and slow the story's pace, so professional short story authors avoid them. Where possible, weave the information about the character's past into the narration, using just a few words here and there. For example, "The curtains and cushions were black, like those in her brother's bedroom when he went through his Goth phase."

HOW TO SHORTEN AN OVER-LONG STORY

Perhaps you've already written a draft, and you need to shave off wordage to get it below the maximum word count for the anthology to which you want to submit. Or maybe your beta readers tell you that your story drags and needs tightening.

Follow the six techniques I've outlined above. They'll help you get the word count down drastically. It's more work to apply them in retrospect than if you had used them from the start, but they bring results.

Cut introspections. Whenever your point of view character spends a lot of time thinking, pondering, wondering, assessing, evaluating, remembering, reminiscing, musing and emoting, cut the lot. Condense all the thoughts in that scene into two sentences. The character's actions will reveal much of her thinking process anyway.

Delete superfluous words. Many words carry little or no meaning; you can shed them without loss. Here are the main candidates: could, start/started to, begin/began to, that, then, somewhat, somehow, really, completely, very, say, all, just. For example, "She could hear a cock starting to crow" (8 words) could become "She heard a cock crow" or even "A cock crowed." (3 words)

NOVICE MISTAKE TO AVOID

Inexperienced writers often write far more material than the tale needs, including character backstories, world-building, historical and geographic information. In itself, this is not bad: it allows you to feel your way into the story, to get to know the characters and places. Just remember to trim those superfluous parts in the final version.

PROFESSIONAL TIP

Save the sections you've cut, and put them in a file. One day, you may want to create a longer version of the same story, perhaps to submit it to an anthology or contest which has a different word-count requirement. Then you can look at the cut bits and decide which of them you want to put back in.

The techniques I've outlined in this chapter are suggestions, not rules. Although they work for most stories, not all of them may be right for the tale you want to tell. View them as helpful signposts pointing in what's probably the best direction. If your plot needs to go elsewhere, follow your vision.

CHOOSE THE SETTING: LOCATION, WEATHER, ATMOSPHERE

Where does your story take place? Consult the list you created for the Chapter 1 assignment. It contains several fascinating places, and one of them may be perfect for this yarn.

Consider giving your story an unusual, quirky setting. This will make the piece memorable and vivid. What's the weirdest possible place where the events could plausibly happen?

If this is a romantic story about a first date, how about these two people don't go to a predictable meal in a restaurant, walk in a park or movie in a cinema, but a Ferris wheel ride at the funfair, rollerblading in a deserted car park, or picnicking on a mountain top?

Could the story perhaps happen in an abandoned factory warehouse, a wine cellar, a sauna, a horse stable, a hayloft, a mineshaft, a cable car, a children's playground, a stalactite cave? The more unusual, the better.

Consider putting all the characters into a 'locked room' – a single enclosed place from which they cannot escape. This intensifies the tension. Consider a railway carriage, a cable car, a prison cell, a cave with a blocked entrance, an island surrounded by shark-infested waters, a mountain hut during a blizzard... If the characters have no choice but to stay, everything becomes more intense.

A story may have more than one setting. Perhaps it starts in the kitchen, then moves into the garden, then the neighbour's house, and finally back into the kitchen. However, it's best to keep to as few places as possible, because if you keep hopping locations, your story may grow unwieldy and long.

CREATING ATMOSPHERE

Skilled descriptions of the setting create intense atmosphere.

Lengthy setting descriptions can be boring, and readers are prone to skip those paragraphs, so it's best to keep the descriptions short but intense.

Here are four techniques I want you to try.

1. What's the weather like? Intense weather – blizzard, heat wave, downpour, deep fog – can add interest to any story. It can also strain characters' tempers, increase tensions, intensify passions and foil plans. Write one or two sentences, describing the weather from the PoV's perspective. Also show how it affects the PoV's experience: are the rain-slick roads slippery when she needs to run? Does she shiver in her thin dress? Does the heat glue her blouse to her chest?

2. Describe the source, quality, colour or intensity of the light. This works superbly to create mood, and it can also help to establish the time of the day. Try to filter the impression through the PoV character's mood.

3. Of all the senses, smell has the most descriptive power. The mere mention of a smell is enough to pull the reader into the scene. A single sentence about smells creates more atmosphere and reveals more about the place than several paragraphs of visual descriptions.

    As an experiment, just read these pairings and see what images they conjure up in your mind:

    The room smelled of...

    ... disinfectant and boiled cabbage

… patchouli and beeswax

… mothballs and lavender

… pizza and unwashed socks

I suggest combining two or three smells, perhaps in this format: 'The air/room/place smelled/reeked/stank of XYZ and ZYX'. Put this sentence near the beginning of your story, or when the PoV just enters the place.

4. Sounds add excitement. They can also create suspense and increase tension. Where possible, use vivid verbs to describe the sounds. Here are some examples:

Computers beeped, phones shrilled, and printers whirred.

A shutter banged against the frame.

A car door slammed. A motor whined.

A dog howled in the distance.

Waves hissed against the shore.

Rodent feet scurried.

Water gurgled in the drainpipe.

NOVICE MISTAKE TO AVOID

Inexperienced writers tend to use generic settings and nondescript weather, missing out an opportunity to make their stories vivid.

PROFESSIONAL TIP

Change the weather during the story. If it's sunny at the beginning of the tale, let it rain later. If it rains at the start, cease the rain and show sunshine and perhaps a rainbow. Increase the gentle dance of snowflakes to a fierce snow storm, and turn up the temperature from pleasant warmth to unbearable heat.

This technique adds interest to any story.

ASSIGNMENT

Choose the setting (or settings) for your story. Jot down at least one smell and three sounds per setting.

Decide on the weather, and whether it will change or remain the same.

ASSIGNMENT

If you have a story draft which is too long for its intended market, or feels 'dragging', apply the techniques I've described here.

Otherwise, look at the story you're currently working on. Would it benefit from one of the described techniques to make it tighter and stronger?

CHAPTER 13

DIALOGUE: SIZZLING AND REALISTIC

Now the story is ready for your attention to detail, so let's look at how to craft dialogue.

The secret to great dialogue: the characters don't talk the way their authors do.

LET THE PERSONALITY SHINE THROUGH

List the characters in your story. For each, choose three adjectives describing their personality. You have already done this for the main character in Chapter 6. Now do it for the others. (At this stage, you probably know your characters well enough to do this.)

How would a person with these characteristics talk? What kind of speech patterns reflect this personality?

Examples:

A self-centred person probably uses the words 'I', 'my' and 'me' a lot.

A timid person may preface requests and statements with an apology: "I'm sorry to bother you. I wonder if it's possible to..." "I'm probably wrong, but..."

An insecure person may use 'maybe', 'perhaps'.

A bossy person may phrase many sentences as a command. "Take a taxi." "Call me tomorrow."

A status-seeking person may name-drop and mention status symbols at every opportunity; "Last week, the Duchess told me..." "When I parked my Porsche..."

A pompous person may speak in multisyllabic words.

Inventing speech patterns can be real fun. Enjoy!

Consider the person's level of education. A high-school drop-out uses a different vocabulary than a PhD graduate. How 'educated' is the speech? Add a note to the list of this character's speech patterns.

HOW TO WRITE GREAT DIALOGUE

- To make fiction dialogue vivid, write it as tightly as possible, cutting superfluous words. One-liners have great impact.

- To make fiction dialogue sound real, use short sentences. Real life dialogue often rambles on in long sentences, but fictional dialogue comes across as more real if the sentences are short.

- To make fiction dialogue exciting, use questions. Questions hook the reader's interest more than statements. Let the characters talk in questions as much as possible.

- To make dialogue sizzling, let characters answer questions with questions. Each time a question is answered with another question, the tension rises.

- Use tags (he said, she asked, he replied) only when they're needed for clarity of who's talking. If the characters are busy doing things, then you can simply write their spoken sentences before or after the action, and it's clear who's talking. For example:

Mary turned the tap off. "What now?"

NOVICE MISTAKE TO AVOID

New writers often use dialogue tags where none are needed. Here are two examples:

"This is not acceptable," John said, rising to leave.

Mary checked her make-up in the mirror. "Will Carlos be there?" she asked.

Without the tag, the meaning of these sentences is just as clear, but stronger:

"This is not acceptable." John rose to leave.

Mary checked her make-up in the mirror. "Will Carlos be there?"

PROFESSIONAL TIP

Let the characters do something while they talk. Give them a job, a task, an assignment, whether it's washing the dishes or cracking a safe.

ASSIGNMENT

Write a dialogue between two characters in your story. If you have a draft for this already, you can use and refine it. Aim to reveal some personality traits in how the characters talk, and try to include at least two questions.

CHAPTER 14

SHORT STORY ENDINGS TO AVOID

Certain short story endings almost inevitably lead to rejection. What are they, and why should you avoid them?

1. *"And then I woke up. It was only a dream"*

You've created an exciting story, and your readers sit on the edge of their seat to await the outcome... and then you reveal that none of it happened. What a let-down!

In my role as an anthology editor and contest judge, I've received quite a few of those, mostly from novice writers who are submitting their first stories. Other editors and writing contests judges are fed up with them, too. Often, when I chat with editors and judges, one of them says, "Today I got a big batch of 'it was only a dream' submissions," and the rest of us just roll our eyes and groan in sympathy.

The ending should always be more exciting than what came beforehand, not less.

2. *It was only a game, a computer simulation, a rehearsal, a drill*

This is similar to the 'dream' ending, because it invalidates the story and delivers disappointment instead of excitement. A better variation has the readers (and the characters) believe that it's a game, and they discover that the danger is real – but this twist has also been done many times already.

3. *The supposed monster is harmless*

The writer leads the readers to believe that the main character is being pursued or threatened by an evil creature, a serial killer or a zombie... but in the end, it turns out to be a harmless stranger, a fellow police officer, Grandmother, the neighbour's friendly dog or the narrator's own shadow.

I still remember a wonderfully exciting story I read as a contest judge twenty years ago. A young woman was walking alone down a street at night, and realised she was being pursued. The author built the suspense with such skill that I felt my heart thud in my throat and was convinced that I had found the winning story. Then the character turned around discovered that the pursuer was the neighbour's friendly dog. How I wished that this author had used her writing skills to craft a powerful ending instead of using a cop-out!

4. *"Their names were Adam and Eve"*

This is an overused ending especially in the Science Fiction genre. A man and a woman in a spacecraft – usually the only survivors of a cataclysm – land on a habitable planet. The final sentence of the story reveals their names: Adam and Eve.

This twist would be clever and funny if thousands of writers hadn't thought of it already. Some science fiction zines even state in their Guidelines for Contributors: "No Adam and Eve stories, please."

5. *The gibberish death*

In a journal entry or letter, the character narrates how he tries to avoid a problem (usually a disease, radiation, parasite or pollution threaten to affect the brain). He believes he has been successful in evading the danger, but his writing becomes increasingly garbled. In the final paragraph, it's pure gibberish and ends abruptly.

This is a great story idea – but unfortunately, thousands of writers have had the same idea already.

6. *The character has been dead all along*

The reader follows the story in which the narrator tries to avoid getting killed. The final paragraph reveals that he has been dead all along.

Readers can usually guess this twist long before the end.

7. *The bite-hider*

Two close friends or a couple of lovers struggle to escape from a horde of zombies or vampires, and experience hair-raising danger and several near misses. At the end of the story, just when they can finally feel safe, one friend turns to his companion, opens his mouth – and bares fangs. He's been bitten and turned into a vampire/zombie himself, but hid it successfully until now.

Fantasy editors get a lot of bite-hider stories.

8. *He's a she, or she's a he*

Told in first person, these stories use gender stereotypes to fool the reader. The narrator talks about working as a nurse, picking the children up, cooking dinner for the family. Naturally, the reader assumes this is a woman, but the final paragraph reveals that the character is a man. Sometimes it's the other way round, and the firefighter/builder/army general turns out to be a woman.

Using short stories to challenge gender stereotypes can be a good strategy – but a 'ha-ha, fooled you' ending achieves nothing but irritation.

9. *God is a computer*

In science fiction stories, a group of people or a whole society worship a god who tells them what to do. Obedience repeatedly saves them from disaster, and they practise complex rituals to keep the god's favour. In the end, the main character comes face to face with this god – and it's a sophisticated computer.

The first of these stories were published 100 years ago. Nowadays, computers are so common that many writers think of this twist, and readers are no longer surprised.

10. *The computer becomes a god*

In a variant of the 'god is a computer' story, the characters are aware that the omniscient entity is a computer – but in the end, it becomes a god.

Stories of this type boomed for a short time in the middle of the twentieth century – then readers grew tired of them. Don't try to flog this dead horse.

11. *"The next day, I read in the paper that my friend had died"*

The narrator has a weird experience involving a far-away friend or relative. He shakes off the hallucination – and the next day he learns that the friend had died at the exact time of the communication.

This plot twist was a staple in Victorian Ghost stories. If you use it now, it will elicit a mere yawn.

12. *And then everyone died*

After struggling valiantly to survive (a pandemic, a terror attack, a zombie apocalypse), everyone gets killed anyway.

For the readers, this is frustrating, because they have rooted for the characters for the whole of the story, so it's a let-down to learn that it was all in vain.

Novice writers often seek to shock readers with this ending. I confess that when I was new to fiction writing, I penned one of those stories myself, believing the ending to be clever and profound.

NOVICE MISTAKE TO AVOID

Most novice writers pen at least one of those stories, unaware that many other writers have had the same idea already. Don't take it to heart – the time you spent on this was not completely wasted, because creating the story was still a useful exercise and helped you grow as a writer.

PROFESSIONAL TIP

Instead of forcing a twist at the end, simply focus on creating a strong ending, one which will leave an emotional impact on the reader. You can always add a surprising element to the ending.

ASSIGNMENT

Think about a short story you've read whose ending you found disappointing. Why did those endings not work? Was it an anticlimax? Did the twist feel forced? Did the plot just fizzle out? Try to pinpoint the reason these story didn't work, because this will teach you what to avoid in your own tales.

CHAPTER 15

WRITING A HALLOWEEN STORY

A Halloween story has two characteristics: it must unfold on or around the time of Halloween, and it must be scary in some way. Here are some ideas and tips for creating your own scary Halloween story.

1. The story features a Halloween ritual – but not necessarily a predictable one

The story plot needs to involve Halloween customs or rituals. However, these don't need to be the conventional trick-or-treating, carved pumpkins and fancy-dress costumes. Consider the seasonal traditions of other cultures, regions and religions and draw on them for inspiration.

For example, in Italy people turn cemeteries into stunning displays of colour by leaving chrysanthemums on graves – not only the graves of loved ones, but those of strangers. What if someone decorates a stranger's grave, and encounters either the ghost of the deceased or a living relative? At the annual Halloween pageant in Kawasaki (Japan) only select people may participate, and competition is fierce. How far will someone go to be among those included in the pageant this year?

Also think of the Día de los Muertos in Mexico with its manifold customs. Families bring the favourite toys of deceased children to their graves. What if they are mistaken about what toy a child truly liked and bring the wrong one? What if the dead child in the adjoining grave is jealous of the offerings?

Consider the ancient Celtic holiday of Samhain, still celebrated in Scotland and Ireland with huge bonfires, carved turnips and masked parades. 31 October marks not only the last day of the harvest and the beginning of the Celtic New Year, but is also the date when the veil between this world and the Otherworld is at its thinnest. This is the time to look into the future (with scrying and fortune-telling) and to communicate with the dead. It is also the time when evil spirits can enter this realm and possess people and animals, so many rituals exist to ward off demons. What if a character communicates with a departed loved one and opens the gates to invite him back into her life – and in doing so accidentally lets in an evil demon?

2. Draw on your own memories of the days around Halloween

How did your family celebrate it when you were a child? Have you lived abroad and experienced different seasonal traditions?

In Germany, where I grew up, children hollowed out not pumpkins but fodder beets, whose flesh is much harder and more difficult to carve. Year after year, I begged to be allowed to make a 'Rübengeist', but my parents refused. Then one year, they gave me a fodder beet and a kitchen knife, and left me to it. I spent hours whittling away at the beet, my cold-stiffened fingers clasped around the knife, chiselling out one wet pale flake after another. When I realised that carving a Rübengeist was tedious work, I wished there was a way to get it done faster. What if someone – a ghost, the devil, an evil human – appears and offers to hollow out the beet fast, in return for a favour, of course?

3. How to find your story's plot

What happens to set the story events in motion? Let it be a seasonal incident, for instance Halloween custom (e.g. two mums competing whose child will have the best costume), perhaps a deliberate dare among young people ("I dare you to spend Halloween in that haunted ruin"), the weather (e.g. a character seeking shelter from an autumn storm) or a communication with the Otherworld (scrying to see the future, using an Ouija board or summoning a spirit).

What can possibly go wrong with the characters' plans? Let it go disastrously wrong, and leave the characters to cope with the fiasco as best they can. This will be your story's plot.

4. Make it Scary

A Halloween story must be scary in some way – but how scary is up to you. If you want to write a tale so terrifying that it scares your readers out of their wits, go for it. But you can also weave a tale which invokes the subtler flavours of fear, i.e. apprehension, dread and suspense. Whether you pen a splatterpunk story filled with gore and violence, a creepy atmospheric Ghost story, or a tongue-in-cheek black humour piece, is your choice. Create the kind of story which suits your author brand and your personal taste.

What kind of horror story would you enjoy reading? Subtle or extreme? That's the style you should aim for in your writing.

5. It Doesn't Have to be Horror

Although a Halloween story has Horror elements, it can be of any genre: Humour, Romance, Mystery... Pen your Halloween story in the genre you like best, just flavour it with creepiness or fear.

6. How to Begin the Story

Don't start with a terrifying situation or a full-on shock, otherwise there's no way left to escalate the fear. The first paragraphs should set the scene and evoke a creepy atmosphere and introduce a disquieting sense of dread, apprehension or suspense, but not yet outright terror.

7. Build the Fear Gradually

With every page, the story becomes scarier. Turn on the volume of fear gradually, escalating it when the tale reaches its climax.

A good way to achieve this gradual build-up is to let the character realise the danger bit by bit. At first, he thinks of it as a disturbing nuisance. Then he gets worried that there may be more to it than he thought. When he realises the magnitude of the danger, he wishes he could turn back, but it's too late. Of course the threat turns out to be much, much worse than what he imagines.

8. What is Real, What is Fake?

With a Halloween story, you can keep the main character (and your readers) in uncertainty about what is real and what is fake. He may cling to the hope that the horrific sight of corpses on his neighbour's lawn is merely a clever Halloween decoration, and that the cellar door locking behind him is merely his mates playing a prank on him. Of course, he'll soon learn better – but even then, reality and illusion intermingle. For example, he may snatch up an axe to use in defence against the monster and find that it's a toy made from foam. Or perhaps he drags himself, injured and bleeding, into the street and begs passers-by to call an ambulance – and they laugh, believing it to be a Halloween gag.

9. How to End the Story

A Halloween story can have a happy or unhappy ending, or anything in between. The main character may escape from the threat and defeat the monster, emerging a wiser and better person than he used to be – or he may pay for his foolishness with his life, realising with his dying breath what a mistake he made.

But it must not end with an anticlimax, showing that the danger was not real. Don't disappoint your readers by revealing that it was only a scary-looking Halloween decoration, a misunderstanding, or a trick-or-treating prank.

10. Use the Weather

The weather is a great way to create atmosphere, establish a seasonal flavour and bring a story to life, especially if the story is set out of doors. Do golden leaves dance in the autumn breeze, or do the brown leaves turn to mush in the gutter? Does rain soak the character's fancy-dress costume, or does the fierce chilly wind bite her cheeks? Do her steps sink into the muddy ground or slip on the frozen pavement?

11. Use the Senses

The ancient Greeks believed there were only five senses (sight, sound, smell, taste and touch), but actually there are many more. Use whichever senses work in the context of your story, and use them a lot. Don't rely on the sense of sight alone. In a Halloween story, the sense of hearing is especially effective because it creates excitement, enhances creepiness and intensifies fear. Describe the sound of a door squealing open or clanking shut, of footsteps thudding on the steps or clacking along the corridor, of stairs creaking and shutters banging. Another great sense to apply in a Halloween story is the sense of temperature. Turn the temperature up or down to make your characters shiver or sweat.

12. Play with Light and Darkness

Describe the source and quality of light: the jaundiced glow of the street lamps, the cold white glare of the bare light bulb, the flickering neon tube overhead. Let the readers experience darkness descending as day surrenders to night, as the candle burns out, as the power cut plunges everything into darkness. Show shadows dancing, creeping, sneaking across floors and walls, lengthening, stretching, reaching. This helps to create a wonderfully creepy atmosphere.

NOVICE MISTAKE TO AVOID

Don't try to shock the reader with a terrifying beginning. This would leave you with nothing to build up to. As an editor of Horror story anthologies and judge of Horror writing contests, I've received many submissions with this flaw. Instead, start the story with a sense of unease and foreboding, and gradually build up the fear.

PROFESSIONAL TIP

At the end of October, surrounded by Halloween customs and drenched in seasonal weather experiences, it's easy to get in the mood. Observe, research, experience, take notes and start writing your story now. This will give you time to revise, edit and polish your tale and submit it to zines and anthologies in time for next year's Halloween issues.

ASSIGNMENT

Get Artist Brain on the job. Do a twenty-minute freewrite, as instructed in the chapter 'Freewriting: Just Let it Flow' about your memories, experiences and thoughts regarding Halloween.

After twenty minutes, take a break, then read what you've written and highlight the interesting bits.

CHAPTER 16

HOW TO WRITE A SPOOKY GHOST STORY

Ghost stories have always been reader favourites. They appeal to a wider audience than most other stories: children enjoy them as much as adults. Even people who normally cringe at the thought of Horror fiction gain pleasure from a good ghostly yarn. How can you write an entertaining, creepy story?

PLOT AND BACKSTORY

All good Ghost stories consist of two tales. The first is the past tragedy which keeps the ghost haunting in search of atonement or vengeance. The second is about the person whose life gets thrown off course when the ghost intervenes.

The Ghost story needs more pre-planning than most other dark fiction, because you need to weave these two strands together.

The human's story which takes place in the current time is probably the main plot. The ghost's story is 'backstory', revealed perhaps in dialogue when the ghost talks, or in the narrative when the human researches the history of the place.

A common plot for a Ghost story is this: a character hears about a haunted house, derides the superstition, and spends a night there to disprove the existence of the ghost. The ghost is real and so terrifying that the character is glad to get away with his life, and never mocks ghosts again. Many fine Ghost stories are built on this basic plot. If you choose to develop this premise, try to come up with a fresh angle.

However, you can use your own ideas for an unusual storyline. With Ghost stories, almost anything goes.

CHOOSING THE LOCATION

You may want to set your story in a creepy place – a cemetery, a castle ruin, a dilapidated mansion, an abandoned mineshaft or dungeon – or you can surprise the reader by placing the haunting in a setting that's not normally considered spooky: a bingo hall, a family car, a grocer's shop, a children's playground, a hotel's swimming pool. Unusual settings will make your story stand out, which can be important when entering a writing contest or submitting to an anthology.

Most hauntings are tied to locations, especially the places where they lived, died or are buried. Old inns, WWII airfields and theatres are among the most haunted places. Choosing one of these settings will give your story believability.

Whatever setting you select for your Ghost story – traditional, surprising or probable – it's up to you to make it creepy.

CREATING SPOOKY EFFECTS

Ghost stories flourish when you create a creepy atmosphere. The following techniques work especially well for Ghost stories:

Darkness, lights and shadows

Show night falling, lightbulbs flickering, shadows dancing across walls.

Sounds

Describe background noises – leaves rustling, shutters banging, a dog howling – the thud of the living character's own footsteps, and eerie effects like creaking stairs and screeching door hinges.

Chills

Play with the effects of temperature. When the air grows cold and the character feels the chills, the readers will shiver with her. In real-life haunted places, the spot where the ghost appears is often inexplicably colder than the surroundings – perhaps this is an effect you can use.

The mood of most Ghost stories is creepy throughout. Humorous Ghost stories are also popular.

THE CAST OF CHARACTERS

The story will have at least two characters who interact with one another – a living human and a ghost. Depending on the story's length, you can add one or several additional characters.

WHO IS THE POINT-OF-VIEW?

The natural point of view for a Ghost story is the human who meets the ghost. However, you can surprise your readers by telling the story from the ghost's perspective, giving them the unique experience of being 'inside' a ghost.

UNDERSTANDING THE GHOST

The ghost haunts because she needs something, and she can find no rest until this is achieved. What does she need? It may be something benign, such as revealing the location of the treasure to the right person or making amends for an atrocity, but it can also be something terrible, such as exacting vengeance and killing the last surviving member of a certain family.

Who is this character? Why does she haunt? What does she need? What does she do to get this? In what way does this particular human hold the key to her fulfilment?

FLESHING OUT THE HUMAN CHARACTER

The living human wants something, too – perhaps related to either the ghost or the place. What does the human want, why does he want it, and why is he trying to get it at this time in this place? If the setting is an abandoned building or a remote location at night, you need to give him a good reason to be there.

How does the human feel about ghosts? Does he believe in them? How does he feel about this particular ghost?

NOVICE MISTAKE TO AVOID

Beginner writers often forget to give the ghost a goal and motivation.

PROFESSIONAL TIP

You can give the story depth if the needs of the ghost and the human are related, especially if the human is about to make the same mistake the ghost once made, or has a similar guilty secret. Ideally, the human grows as a result of the encounter, and becomes a wiser, better person.

ASSIGNMENT

Choose a location – perhaps one from the list of places you created earlier, perhaps a different one. Now ask yourself, who might haunt here, and why? What living human might come here, and why? What will happen if the human and the ghost meet?

Next, choose one of two approaches: either do a twenty-minute freewrite (with Artist Brain in charge) or, if you feel more comfortable with tight constructions, go straight to plot events structuring.

CHAPTER 17

HOW TO WRITE A HEARTWARMING CHRISTMAS STORY

Every year, magazines, e-zines, anthologies, websites, newspapers and other publications are looking for stories to include in their edition for the festive season. December is the ideal time to write a Christmas story, because you're surrounded by seasonal weather, decorations and activities. Getting into the mood and finding ideas is easy. Once you've penned the complete draft, you can revise and edit your tale in time to submit for next year's Christmas editions.

WHAT MAKES A CHRISTMAS STORY GREAT?

1. The story has a feel-good factor and a heart-warming plot

Readers want uplifting stories to read over the holiday season, so that's what editors are looking for. Depressive and cynical works with unhappy endings would be difficult to sell, but heart-warming yarns are in demand. See if you can pen a tale that makes readers sigh contentedly at the end.

2. The story is set at or around Christmas

This includes Christmas Eve, Christmas Day and Boxing Day, and also the season of Christmas preparations (e.g. Advent) and the seasonal holidays of other cultures and religions, i.e. Kwanzaa, the Winter Solstice or Hanukkah.

3. The story is thoughtful

The readers learn something new – perhaps about social issues or personal relationships – and are encouraged to ask themselves how they would have acted in the main character's place, whether their own choices and actions would be up to the mark. Stories without message and depth are unlikely to find a buyer. But stories which make the readers think are winners.

4. The plot revolves around a Christmas-related value

The story explores and promotes a human value that is related to the Christmas spirit. Typical values interpreted in Christmas stories are compassion, kindness, generosity, tolerance, hope, forgiveness and peace. Often, the main character (MC) learns the true meaning of one of those values, and the readers gain the insight through him.

5. The story deals with real issues in a realistic way

Although the story can have fantasy and paranormal elements (e.g. a Ghost story), it needs to be grounded in realism. It presents a truthful snapshot of a social issue (such as poverty, homelessness, unemployment, war, racism, abandoned animals, destruction of nature) or personal problem (i.e. loneliness, divorce, cancer, mental illness, disability, suicide).

6. The story has a positive outcome for at least two characters

Your tale needs to end on a positive note. At least two of the characters are in a better situation afterwards. Perhaps the homeless man has found a job and a place to stay, and the MC who brought it about has finally found peace in her heart. Maybe the starving stray mama cat and her helpless kittens got adopted, and the lonely little girl can finally laugh because she has someone to love and play with. The Christmas story doesn't pretend to solve everyone's problems – it doesn't show an end to poverty, homelessness and war – but it shows that it is possible for individuals to lift themselves and others out of misery.

A BASIC STORY PLOT YOU CAN USE

Here is a plot blueprint you can use to write your own Christmas story.

The MC has a character flaw of which he is not aware, for example, he may be intolerant, greedy, bigot, selfish or cruel. He is particularly hard towards a certain group of people he despises, e.g. the homeless, the unemployed, those of other races or religions. Show him treating those people with disdain.

Something bad happens to him, e.g. a cherished hope he'd held gets dashed, someone on whom he counted lets him down, something he'd taken for granted is taken away from him.

When another bad thing happens (another hope dashed, another person lets him down, another unexpected loss), he sinks into despair.

Then a member of the group he despised offers him a gesture of kindness which he rejects with disdain. But when he is rock-bottom with his despair, the person rescues him (literally or metaphorically).

Now he opens his heart a little and does a small kindness for that person or someone else of that group, and he is surprised at how good this feels.

He makes a bigger gesture, and for the first time experiences the kind of happiness that comes with generosity (or with compassion, or tolerance, or whatever value your story promotes).

He realises what a selfish/greedy/bigot/intolerant/whatever idiot he has been. With this insight, he changes and becomes a better and wiser man. He and the person who rescued him become friends who support each other, and together they set out to help others. End the story by showing how the MC has changed.

Although I've used 'he' for the main character, naturally this could be a female.

Of course, this is just a template which you need to bring to life in your personal way, otherwise it would feel as bland as a piece of cardboard. Infuse it with your own values (what matters to you – religious tolerance, generosity, compassion...?) and real life social issues you care about (do you feel for the plight of homeless people, laboratory animals or refugees?). Enrich it with your personal experiences. (Have you ever worked for a charity that aids homeless people, talked with a homeless person, or lived rough yourself? Have you volunteered in an animal shelter or befriended refugees?) Choose an interesting location (preferably one you know well) and flesh out the characters to make the story uniquely yours.

Feel free to deviate from the blueprint, replacing parts with your original ideas.

CHRISTMAS STORIES FOR EVERY GENRE

Whatever genre you enjoy writing in, you can use it for a Christmas story.

Do you write Romance? Then let the MC and the person she despises learn to respect and then love each other.

Is Horror your genre? Then you may want to follow the tradition of Christmas Ghost stories.

Do you write Cosy Mystery fiction? Then your sleuth may investigate who stole the gift of precious jewellery or who murdered their eccentric host.

For Christian Inspirational fiction, you may want to let the MC (and the readers) learn to see beyond the trappings of the seasonal festivities and come to understand the true Christmas message. Or perhaps the MC starts out as a bigoted person who believes there is only one way to celebrate Christmas, and he learns to widen his heart and become more tolerant and inclusive.

FOR A VIVID EXPERIENCE, INVOLVE THE WEATHER

To create a seasonal atmosphere describe the weather – icicles hanging from roof gutters, snow piling on fence posts, hail hammering against the window, flames prattling in the fireplace. These descriptions don't need to be long, simply insert a descriptive sentence here and there.

If you can, make the weather part of the plot. The homeless people huddle under their folded cardboard boxes, trying to keep warm in the freezing cold. The hiking couple get caught in a snowstorm and seek shelter in a barn.

SENSORY ENRICHMENT

Every story benefits from evoking the senses. For a Christmas story, the most powerful sense is that of smell. Sprinkle smells liberally across your story, and the readers will feel they're experiencing the scene instead of just reading it. Here are some ideas:

Gingerbread, roasted chestnuts, beeswax, candle smoke, pine resin, mulled wine, frankincense, the gifted perfume, the stray dog's wet fur, wood smoke, roast meat, brandy...

NOVICE MISTAKE TO AVOID

New writers often write stories expressing their disillusionment and cynicism about the festive seasons. While such outpourings have therapeutic value for the author, they're almost impossible to sell.

Instead, use your cynicism and disillusionment as a starting point and show how Christmas could become meaningful to someone.

PROFESSIONAL TIP

Focus on what Christmas means to you. What positive values does (or should) Christmas represent? Express this in your story.

ASSIGMENT

This is another job for Artist Brain. Set your timer for twenty minutes, and do a freewrite, pouring all your Christmas-related resentments, disillusionments, conflicts, frustrations, anger and hurt onto the paper.

After a long break (perhaps a day or more) return to what you've written. Underline everything that has the potential to be turned into a story, that can be contrasted with a positive, or solved by a character growing wiser.

Allow yourself another break, then pick one of the underlined items and do a freewrite about this. You will probably feel a story wanting to come out.

CHAPTER 18

HOW TO WRITE A SHORT STORY SPIN-OFF FROM YOUR NOVEL

This chapter is for authors who have published, or are planning to publish, at least one novel. If you are interested in short stories only, you can skip this section.

Do you want to create short stories as spin-offs from your novel? This can be a great marketing strategy. When readers discover your short story on your website or in an anthology, and love it, they will look for more fiction by this author. This can strengthen your reputation as an author and boost your novel's sales.

CAN YOU USE THE NOVEL'S MAIN CHARACTER FOR SPIN-OFF STORIES?

Perhaps you can create a story featuring your novel's main character. After all, you know him well and are familiar with his goals, habits and dilemmas. Readers who love the story will be happy to discover there's a whole novel about this character, and are likely to click the 'buy' button.

Featuring a novel character in short spin-offs works especially well for series. Fans will be delighted to discover a story they can read until the next volume in the series comes out. Famous fiction characters from novel series who appeared in short stories include Lee Child's Jack Reacher, Agatha Christie's Miss Marple and Hercule Poirot, Arthur Conan Doyle's Sherlock Holmes, Sara Paretsky's V.I. Warshawski, Sue Grafton's Kinsey Millhone, Dorothy L. Sayers' Lord Peter Wimsey and Lisa Gardner's Detective D.D. Warren.

Besides being all series characters, the examples have something else in common: they are all sleuths of some kind. This is because most Thrillers and Mysteries are typically more plot-driven than character-driven and lend themselves to spin-offs revolving around their main characters more than other genres do.

You can easily let the series sleuth solve some minor mysteries between the novels, using the same strategies and showing the same quirky habits. Keep in mind that the limited space of a short story requires a much simpler plot with fewer suspects. In a novel, your detective may hunt a serial killer and investigate fifteen suspects. In a story, she's more likely to unravel which of the three suspects stole the diamond brooch.

With other, more character-driven genres, you may face a dilemma. In fiction with psychological depth, the character learns, grows and changes. The character's change in the short story may clash with his growth in the novel.

The situation is even trickier in Romance fiction. Readers want the main character to find their one true love. If you show him finding the love of his life in the short story, the readers won't be happy if the novel features him courting someone else.

If you want to avoid the main character's development in the novel and the short story clashing, here are possible solutions:

- Make the short story a prequel to the novel, featuring the main character's earlier adventures. Let's say your novel is a swashbuckling Epic Fantasy in which the MC goes on a dangerous quest to fight the evil overlord. Then the short story could show him in his youth, learning sword-fighting skills or defeating a minor villain.

- Use the novel's main character as a minor character in the story, because a minor character doesn't need to change. Let's say your novel is a Romance, in which the MC found her true love and married him. In the short story she makes an appearance in a minor role, perhaps as the main character's sister, bridesmaid, work colleague or best friend.

However, my favourite solution is this:

PROMOTE THE SUPPORTING CAST TO LEAD ROLES IN THE SPIN-OFF

This is a safe and fun solution. Minor characters from your novel are perfect candidates for short stories. Who are the interesting, quirky, fascinating people in the novel? Think of the ones whom you enjoyed writing, and the ones your fans love.

Could one of them be the star of a short story?

You know the character already and don't need to develop him from scratch. This saves time. Readers who love the character in the story will be happy to hear he's part of a novel, and fans of the novel will enjoy reading a tale featuring their favourite sidekick. The character can grow and change during the short story without affecting the novel series' story line.

Start by making a list of the minor characters in your novel. Highlight the ones you enjoyed working with, and also the ones for whom you got enthusiastic feedback from beta-readers, book reviewers and fans.

Choose one of them. What did she want to achieve in the novel? Did she get it? If not, write a story about how she pursues that goal.

What kind of challenge does she face, what difficult situation does she find herself in, what problem does she have in her life that you didn't have room in the novel to explore? This is material for a short story.

The plot of this kind of short story can unfold at the same time as that of the novel, although it's easier to avoid continuity errors if the story takes place after the novel's end.

BENEFITS OF WRITING SPIN-OFF STORIES FROM YOUR NOVEL

- You can submit the short stories to anthologies, where they'll get discovered by genre fans. This will attract new readers to your novel.

- By publishing a short story on your website, you give readers a free sample of your writing. After reading a complete short story, they will know whether or not they want to read more from this author. Add a buy-link to your novel, so those who love the story can immediately click to buy the book.

- When promoting your novel, you can use a short story as a prize in giveaways. This works better than giving away the novel itself.

- If you are writing a novel series, releasing short stories will keep fans connected and happy until the next novel comes out.

WRITING FAN FICTION STORIES

Instead of creating stories derived from your own novel, you can craft yarns based on someone else's – perhaps a book series, a television show, or a movie. For this, you pick the ready-made settings, characters and situations, and weave your own stories around them. This is 'fan fiction' and fun to write. However, keep in mind that you won't own the copyright to the original material, and this seriously limits what you can do. You can write the story and share it with other fans – but you won't be allowed to sell or publish it.

NOVICE MISTAKE TO AVOID

New writers, tired of working on the novel, often seek variety by writing short stories in an unrelated genre. There's nothing wrong with this – but don't expect a story to attract readers to your novel if it isn't in the same genre.

PROFESSIONAL TIP

Use a scene you deleted from your novel draft and recycle it as a short story. Perhaps you had to cut a scene, a chapter or a whole subplot from your manuscript because they led away from the main plot or because the book was growing too long. Although entertaining and exciting, these sections were not right for the novel and had to go. If you were sad to 'kill your darlings', now you can bring them back to life. With some restructuring, they may become perfect stand-alone stories.

ASSIGNMENT

Which of the supporting characters in your novel is interesting enough to feature in a story of her own? Do a twenty-minute freewrite – from her perspective. Let her talk about her adventures, her ambitions, her problems, her fears. You (with Artist Brain as the intermediary) write down what the character says.

During this exercise, you'll probably feel a story idea forming.

CHAPTER 19

REVISION: IMPROVING YOUR DRAFT

This is the chapter Editor Brain has been waiting for.

By now your story is a real story, so it's ready for revision. It's not publishable yet; that's why it needs revising. Some people call this process 'editing', but 'editing' can mean many different things, so I prefer 'revising' which is specific.

Editor Brain is very good at revising. Send Artist Brain on a well-deserved break and let Editor Brain do the job.

Editor Brain can chop superfluous paragraphs, restructure sentences, prune extraneous words, replace dull words with vivid ones, clear up confusing bits, correct typos, replace repetitions with synonyms, and more.

I suggest you go through your story several times. Perhaps four times:

1. The first time, you correct obvious flaws and errors.

2. The second time you address specific weaknesses, such as the need to tighten wordy wafflings.

3. This time, focus on 'flavour'. Does this story have the mood and atmosphere you're after? If you're writing for a specific publication, does it have what the editors want?

4. Now read it aloud. You will hear flaws you didn't see. You may want to use a text-to-voice app if you have one (basic versions are usually free to use), because a stranger's voice makes flaws even more obvious.

When you've revised the story, send it to your critique partners for feedback. Consider their advice, and apply some of it in your fifth revision round.

HOW TO RECEIVE CRITIQUES

Personally, I love critiques. I always seek as many crits as I can possibly get. However, if you're new to getting critiques, you may feel daunted. What if people don't like your story?

Critiques aren't judgements, they're tools for you to use.

You're in charge of your story. Listen to all the suggestions, consider whether they suit your vision for your story, and choose which ones to apply. Some suggestions will be a good fit, others won't. Often, a suggestion is excellent but not right for this particular story.

Being in charge and choosing the suggestions can be an empowering experience. I always treat critiques like a buffet of food: it's all laid on for me, far more than I need. I pick and choose what I fancy and leave the rest.

If you don't have critique partners yet, join a writers' group whose members give honest, thorough, constructive feedback. Avoid people who demolish your story or your confidence, and don't waste your time with those who give meaningless bland praise.

Online critique groups are useful because they don't depend on the schedule of face-to-face meetings, and they allow you to collect feedback from peers all over the world. Comments from successful authors of the same genre are especially helpful. However, all feedback from writers of all genres can help.

Tell your critique partners if you are hoping to achieve a certain effect with your story, e.g. if you want it to be inspiring, uplifting or scary. They can help you with suggestion how to achieve this.

NOVICE MISTAKE TO AVOID

Some novices avoid constructive feedback, either from fear of criticism, or because they don't want to be 'influenced'. They don't realise that constructive criticism and the influence of peers can help take their stories from 'so-so' to great.

PROFESSIONAL TIP

Get as many critiques as you possibly can, but keep in mind that your partners will expect you to return the favour, so don't over-commit.

ASSIGNMENT

Find at least three writers who will critique your story.

CHAPTER 20

GET YOUR STORY PUBLISHED

We're in a 'golden age' for short stories, with more opportunities for short story authors than ever before. This doesn't mean that getting your tales published is easy, or a way to earn riches fast.

You need to be sure that your stories are good, and you need to submit them to the right markets.

WHERE TO SUBMIT YOUR STORY

If your story falls under a category (a 'genre'), focus on markets specialising in that genre, because there your chances of acceptance are greatest.

If you write Science Fiction, submit to Science Fiction zines. If you write Horror, seek out Horror publications. Their readers want this kind of story, therefore their editors are actively looking.

Most publications have 'Guidelines for Contributors' where they explain what they're looking for – genres, length, flavours and so on. Read those carefully and submit your story only if it matches their requirements.

Several websites offer 'Market Listings', showing which publications are currently open to submission and what they want. My favourite site is Ralan.com, a free-to-use comprehensive site with frequently updated information about markets for speculative fiction, horror and humour.

Find a site listing markets in your genre, and make sure the information is up to date.

Print magazines are a rapidly shrinking market, and your story is unlikely to find a place in one of them. The chances are much bigger with e-zines (aka webzines, or simply 'zines') because this market is expanding and hungry for good fiction.

Anthologies are themed collections with works by several authors. Whether published as ebooks or paperbacks, they are treasured by their buyers who often re-read them several times. In ebook form, they remain published for many years and attract reviews on bookselling sites such as Amazon. If you're listed as one of the authors, there'll be a link to your other books, which will help promote your novel. Getting your story into a quality anthology – preferably one edited by a respected editor and containing stories by established authors – can be a big step in your writing career.

Some markets pay professional rates, others offer semi-professional payment or a token. Since your aim is exposure rather than payment, the level of pay is not important. However, the publications that pay most are usually the ones that offer the best exposure.

Don't be discouraged by rejections. All writers get those. Your story may simply not be what the editor wants at the moment, or perhaps the editor has just accepted a similar story already. However, some publications take months before they decide your story's fate, and it can take years of continuous submission before your story finally finds a home.

CHECK THE RIGHTS

When submitting the story to other people for publication, check what rights they require. Some want 'first rights' (that is, they want to be the first to publish it), and some want 'all rights' (that means, you can't publish it anywhere else).

Don't sign anything until you know which rights you're giving away. Here's a quick run-down of the basics. Disclaimer: I'm not a lawyer and this doesn't constitute professional legal advice.

Non-exclusive

This is ideal. You own all the rights to your story and can use it elsewhere in any way you like. Go for it.

Exclusive for a certain period

This is reasonable. Most magazines and e-zines require this. It means you can't publish the story for a year or whatever that period is, but afterwards, you're free to do with it what you like. If the magazine or e-zine specialises in your genre or reaches many readers who are similar to your Average Reader, it's worth it.

First Serial Rights

This means they don't care what you do with the story afterwards, but they want to be the first. This often comes in combination with 'exclusive for a certain period'. It's acceptable, but needs careful planning, because you can surrender your story's virginity only once. For a prestigious zine, it's worth it. However, pay attention to the Rights Reversal clause. More about that below.

First Regional Serial Rights

Contracts used to be for First North American Serial Rights, First British Serial Rights etc. This has become almost obsolete in the internet age.

Exclusive

Caution! This means you can't publish the story anywhere else, not even on your own website. Some anthologies demand exclusive rights. Agree to this only if it's a very prestigious publication and they offer you a lot of money.

All Rights

Caution! This is similar to 'exclusive' (you won't be able to use your story elsewhere), but it's worse: now they own the story and can even sell it on. Agree to this only in special circumstances – for example, if the zine or anthology is extremely prestigious or if they offer you filthy amounts of money.

Rights Reversal Clauses

What happens if a publication folds? If you own the rights to your story, that's not a big problem, because you can simply submit the piece elsewhere. But if you've signed away the rights, your story may never get published or read.

Many writers get caught out by a contract clause in which they agree to give the publisher exclusive rights until X months after publication. If the publication folds, your story is lost.

To prevent this, most agreements contain a paragraph about 'Rights Reversal' which says that under certain circumstances, the rights will return to the author. Ideally, the clause says something like, 'If the story is not published by X date, all rights will return to the author'.

Be wary of clauses which promise Rights Reversal only if the project is cancelled (because the publisher may never cancel it but simply postpone it for decades), or require the author to write to the publisher to demand the rights (because the project may have been sold to someone else and you may not even know the new publisher's name).

Consider this situation especially if it is a new publication. Many newly-launched projects fail within the first couple of years, often leaving the story rights in limbo.

Hiring a lawyer to vet each short story publication contract may not be practical. However, you should read the Rights Reversal clause carefully. If in doubt, show it to other writers who have experience with contracts, and if necessary, ask the publisher to provide clarification in writing.

EXPOSURE-ONLY MARKETS

Some publications offer 'exposure' in lieu of payment. Are these worth submitting to? Yes and no. If your story is strong, it deserves to get paid. This is not just a matter of money, but of reaching the right readers.

New zines spring up all the time, usually closing within a few months when the wannabe publishers realise how much work it is. They seldom attract many readers beyond the publishers and the handful of authors themselves. If your story gets published in one of those, it will soon be forgotten.

Many failed writers, fed up with rejections, decide to become editors or publishers. They launch a zine or an anthology, just so that they can showcase their own writing and that of their equally unsuccessful writing buddies. The resulting publications, poorly written and poorly edited, attract nothing but derision. Even if your story is the best of the lot, the low overall standard can damage your reputation. If in doubt about a market, research the editor's background, because the editor is responsible for the project's quality. If she or he is respected in the genre, has edited other zines and anthologies or won awards, that's a good sign. If nothing is known about the editor, and no payment is offered, getting published there won't help you much.

However, if you're new to writing and lack the confidence to approach the quality markets, if your stories are nice but not yet great, then these amateur markets can be a good rehearsal space. Just view them as a step on the way to greater things.

NOVICE MISTAKE TO AVOID

Never pay to get your work published. Whether it's called 'reading fee', 'contribution to printing costs' or 'crowdfunding' – just walk away. Real publishers make money from selling their books and zines to real readers, not from charging naïve new writers.

PROFESSIONAL TIP

Make a list of possible markets. Sort them by desirability, with the ones offering the best exposure at the top. Submit your story to the best market first. If it gets rejected, immediately send it to the next market on your list until it finds a home.

ASSIGNMENT

Use a search engine to find market listings. Then draw up a list of markets which publish the kind of story you write. Bookmark the URLs.

If you don't have a story that's quite right for the market, consider writing one.

If the market is currently closed to submissions, make a note when it will reopen, and check back then.

CHAPTER 21

WHY YOU SHOULD SUBMIT YOUR SHORT STORIES TO ANTHOLOGIES

Getting short stories published in anthologies (collections of stories by multiple authors) can be a big stepping stone in your fiction writing career.

Here are the reasons why you should try:

AS A YARDSTICK

If an anthology editor selects your story, it proves that your writing is good enough to be published. New writers can't judge the quality of their own writing, and friends and family aren't unbiased judges either. So if an independent editor chooses your piece over others, it confirms that your writing has reached an important threshold. Of course, some anthologies have higher standards and are more difficult to get into than others. While getting accepted by any anthology is great for a novice, seasoned writers will seek to get into one of the top anthologies of their genre.

FOR VALIDATION

If you have indie-published (self-published) your novel, other people may think you did this because your writing isn't good enough to be selected by a publisher's editor. You can silence them by pointing out the short stories you've had accepted and published in anthologies. This also washes away any self-doubts you may harbour.

TO GET KNOWN IN THE GENRE

Most anthologies focus on one genre, and get read by that genre's avid fans. When your story is included in an anthology, it gets exposure to genre fans, i.e. people who love the kind of fiction you write. This is exactly the audience you want. While reading an anthology, most readers take note of which stories are their favourites, and look for more fiction by those authors. Those who enjoyed your short tale will want to read a whole book by you. This leads to an increase in sales for your book (assuming that you have one published), and builds a fan base which is invaluable for your writing career.

FOR LONG-TERM SUCCESS

Unlike periodical publications (magazines, e-zines, newspapers) which get published and then forgotten, anthologies are books which continue to exist. Most ebooks remain published forever. Paperbacks, even if they are out of print, will remain in people's bookcases and get sold second-hand. This means that the stories contained in anthologies will get read again and again, constantly reaching new audiences. For writers seeking to build an author brand and gain recognition, anthologies work better than periodicals.

TO PUBLISH A STORY MORE THAN ONCE

Most anthologies accept reprints (i.e. previously published stories). This means you can submit your tale over and over and see it published more than once. Great stories often get published five, ten, or even a hundred times. With each publication, the story gets new readers, and your reputation grows.

TO EARN MONEY

Anthology contributors get paid for the use of their story. Top anthologies pay several hundred dollars for a previously unpublished tale. Most anthologies pay less – indeed, many offer just a token payment of $5 or so – but money always comes in handy, and it's a great feeling to get paid for your writing. Remember that you may sell a story more than once, so the payments can add up.

TO NETWORK WITH OTHER GENRE AUTHORS

Once your story has appeared in an anthology, it's worth getting in touch with the other contributors. You may decide to promote the anthology together, to guest on each other's blogs, share each other's social media content, write a story together as co-authors, share a stall at a genre convention, exchange manuscript critiques, share market information and more. Networking with authors in your genre has many benefits.

TO GET SOCIAL MEDIA FOLLOWERS

Most anthologies include an 'About the Author' paragraph. If you mention your Facebook, Twitter etc. ID, readers who loved your story will follow you. They may tell you how much they loved your story (and getting fan mail feels wonderful), and they will see your social media posts about your books and more.

TO BOOST YOUR BOOK'S EXPOSURE

Major bookselling sites like Amazon give more exposure to authors of multiple books, for example with 'Other Books by this Author' displays. As a contributor to an anthology, your name will be listed as one of the authors which makes you immediately an author with multiple books and boosts your exposure. It also provides a new publication which will keep your author name at the front of the algorithms. (Make sure that your author name is listed on sales sites. You may have to ask the publisher to include it.)

TO EXTEND YOUR LIST OF PUBLISHED BOOKS

When readers search for your name on sites like Amazon, they'll be impressed to see a long list of books. Subconsciously, readers assume that an author with a lot of published books must be successful, and therefore must be good. Every anthology inclusion immediately lengthens your list of published books by one title.

TO IMPRESS WITH PUBLISHING CREDENTIALS

If you seek the corporate (traditional) publishing path for your novel, it's great if you can say in your query letter to literary agents and publishers 'My stories have been published in X, Y and Z anthologies.' This shows that other editors have deemed your work worthy of publication, and encourages editors and agents to take a closer look at your offering than they normally would.

NOVICE MISTAKE TO AVOID

Don't submit your stories to low-standard anthologies, with clueless editors and low-quality content. Having your name associated with that kind of book can do your writing career more harm than good.

PROFESSIONAL TIP

Some anthologies are better than others, more difficult to get into but paying more and providing more prestigious publication credits.

Work your way from the top down, by submitting your story to the most desirable market first. If this results in a rejection, submit it to the second-best, and so on. This way, you won't waste a really great story on a negligible market.

ASSIGNMENT

Find out which anthologies, currently open to submissions, are looking for the kind of story you have written or are working on.

CHAPTER 22

HOW TO PUBLISH YOUR OWN SHORT STORY COLLECTION

Do you want to gather your short stories into a book? Here are insider tips for publishing a successful short story collection. Whether you're looking for an agent or publisher, or plan to self-publish, these tips will put you ahead of the game.

STICK TO ONE GENRE

Short story collections sell best if they focus on one genre, for example, romance, fantasy, historical or horror. Collections within a sub-genre are even more popular, e.g. paranormal romance, urban fantasy, mediaeval historical or psychological horror.

This is because most readers look for their next read in their favourite genre. Rather than browsing thousands of published short story collections, they go straight to the 'romance' category, or type 'paranormal romance stories' in the search box.

So if you write both romance and horror stories, don't put them in the same book.

Professional tip: collections within sub-genres – or even sub-sub-genres – have the best chance of getting discovered by readers.

CHOOSE A THEME

Story collections with a theme sell much better than those without one. A theme could be, for example: *Seaside, Mother's Day, Italy* or *Animal Rescue*.

Readers love stories about their favourite subjects. People who are passionate about pets will be drawn to a book with stories of animal rescues, while readers with fond memories of Italy will reach for the collection of stories set in in that country. Themed story collections are also popular as gift books: "What can we give Suzie for her birthday? She's a bookworm and loves the seaside. Let's get her a book with seaside stories!"

Seasonal themes can work well. You could create a collection of stories about Valentine's Day, Easter, Mother's Day, Christmas, Hanukkah, Eid, Beltane or Halloween.

Professional tip: your story collection's success potential will multiply if it has both a genre and a theme.

GET ENOUGH STORIES

In the early days of ebook publishing, small collections with three to five pieces were popular, but over recent years, readers have come to expect more stories in a book. Aim to get at least eight tales for your collection. Better still, get ten, twelve or twenty.

What if you don't have enough stories? Write more!

You may also be able to rewrite some of your old stories so they match the genre. Let's say you need another romance. If you have a horror manuscript which includes a romantic element, consider rewriting that story so the romance aspect is stronger.

Another possibility is to include stories by another author. Perhaps you have a friend who pens stories in the same genre, writes well and would be happy to be included. In this case, you'll be co-authors of the book, e.g. *'Biting Love: Twelve Paranormal Romance Stories* by Suzie Scrybe and Klaus Schreiber.'

Professional tip: if you work with a co-author, put your agreement in writing: responsibilities (who does what), payment (if any) rights (who will own the copyright to the stories). The most practical arrangement is that you own the copyright for the book as a whole, but your co-author keeps the copyright to their stories and is free to publish them elsewhere.

AIM FOR HIGH QUALILTY

Make your stories as good as you can before you publish the book or submit the manuscript to agents and publishers. Don't settle for second-rate work, neither from yourself nor from your co-author.

If you have a co-author, you can critique each other's contributions.

Professional tip: find readers who love that genre, invite them to beta-read the manuscript, and ask for their constructive criticism.

THE BEST ORDER

The first story in the book is the one viewers see when they click the 'look inside' or 'download free sample' buttons. Choose a story that starts with a powerful hook to draw readers in.

The last story leaves the final impression. Pick an emotion-arousing, thought-provoking tale.

Arrange the remaining stories to create a varied rhythm by alternating short pieces with long ones, funny and serious yarns, your contributions and your co-author's.

Professional tip: the first story determines the book's success, because that's the sample the viewers will see before they decide whether to buy the book. It needs to be strong so they click 'Buy Now – but it also needs to be typical of the whole collection, because it builds expectations. Don't risk disappointing your readers.

CHOOSE THE TITLE AND SUBTITLE

Create a title with words that appeal to fans of that genre, preferably one which isn't already in use by another short story collection. If you're stuck for ideas, use one of the story titles as the book title.

Then add a subtitle which clarifies that this is a short story collection and includes the genre and the theme, *e.g. Twelve Seaside Romance Stories* or *Whodunit Mystery Stories from Ireland.*

Professional Tip: what words will people in search of this kind of book type into the search box? Include those words in the subtitle. This will help increase the book's sales.

CASE STUDY

Let's look at one of my own short story collections, *The Bride's Curse: Bulgarian Gothic Ghost and Horror Stories,* and I'll show you how I applied these tips in practice.

The genre is Horror, and the subgenre is Gothic Horror. Although I had ideas for tales in other genres, I decided to stick to Gothic Horror.

All the stories are set in Bulgaria, the country where I live. So 'Bulgaria' became the theme.

At first, I didn't have enough short stories for a collection. Rather than publish a thin book with only a few stories, I decided to wait until I had more.

I considered finding a co-author, but there aren't many authors of horror stories set in Bulgaria – at least not authors who write in the English language – so I dropped that idea. Instead, I hired a Bulgarian artist to create illustrations for the book.

For each story, I wrote several drafts, revising with the help of other writers who provided constructive criticism. Then I got two beta readers who critiqued the complete book.

I put what I thought was a strong and typical story at the start, and an emotional, thought-provoking piece at the end. My beta readers agreed with my choice for the final tale but urged me to open with a different story, and I followed their advice.

For the title, I considered the titles of the stories. 'The Bride's Curse' stuck out because 'bride' and 'curse' are both evocative words, and they match the Gothic vibe.

The subtitle conveys the genre ('Gothic' & 'Horror') and the theme ('Bulgarian'). I added the word 'Ghost' since many readers use 'Ghost Stories' as a search word.

NOVICE MISTAKE TO AVOID

Many new writers, in a hurry to get a book published, und frustrated by editorial rejections, decide to self-publish before they are ready. Self-publishing (indie-publishing) is a viable option, but your book will need to compete against thousands of other short story collections. If you publish too soon – before you have enough stories to fill a book on a specific theme, before you've sharpened your writing skills, before you've revised and edited your tales so they sparkle with the brilliance of diamonds – your book won't stand a chance.

ASSIGNMENT

Look at the short stories you've written, are working on or plan to write, and also at your lists of subject ideas.

For what genre do you have most material? What theme do you have enough ideas for to fill a book?

CHAPTER 23

HOW TO WIN SHORT STORY CONTESTS: INSIGHTS FROM A WRITING COMPETITION JUDGE

Contests are great for short story writers, because they motivate you to create more stories and to revise them until they sparkle like diamonds. If your story wins, you'll gain recognition, validation that your writing is good, a boost for your credentials. You may also reap a cash prize, and perhaps a certificate, trophy or plaque to display.

So how do you make your story stand out in the eyes of the contest judges?

Of course, you need to write a really good story. All the usual guidelines for story writing apply: character, goal, motivation, conflict, structure, dialogue, hook, satisfying ending and more. Unless you've mastered the craft of short story writing, your chances of success are small, and no insider tricks will help.

But here are several steps you can take to draw the judges' attention to your good story and win their favour.

I've been a judge on many writing competitions – sometimes the only judge, more often part of a judging panel – and I know from experience where many writers go wrong. Today, I'm sharing insider tips. Some of them may surprise you.

1. SUBMIT YOUR STORY EARLY

Try to be among the first who submit.

In many competitions, the judges start reading as soon as the entries arrive. At the beginning, there's only a trickle of stories coming in, and every story gets read carefully. Near the closing date, a deluge of entries arrives. The judges have less time to devote to each story, and they're jaded, because they've read the same kind of story so many times already. A good story arriving in the first few days after the contest opens is more likely to make it to the shortlist than an equally good tale arriving on the closing date.

2. STICK TO THE WORD COUNT

If the competition rules stipulate '2,000-3,000 words' then your story must fall into that bracket. This seems obvious, but surprisingly many contestants don't abide by the word count. I've received many entries where the entrants submitted stories just a few words over the limit, e.g. 3,010 words instead of 3,000. Don't think the judges won't notice, or that they will make an exception for you because your story is so brilliant. If your entry exceeds the word count, it won't even get read.

So, spend a few minutes and find words you can shave off before you submit. If the story really can't be told within the given word limit, write a different one.

By the way, the word count refers to the story itself, and doesn't include the story title and author name.

3. DON'T TELL THE JUDGE WHY YOUR STORY DESERVES TO WIN

Some entrants think they can sway judges with a personal plea. They preface their stories with a paragraph begging for the prize. ("Please choose my story. I know it's not very good, but I have a sick husband and seven kids, and my therapist says that winning this contest would be good for my self-esteem.")

The judges are looking for the best story, not for the most needy or deserving citizens. If your entry starts with a personal plea instead of a great story hook, it will get discarded.

4. FOLLOW THE FORMAT

The contest rules will say how to submit your entry: in the body of an email, as an attachment, through a submission site, or printed with double-spacing on white paper. Send it exactly as stipulated.

Surprisingly many entrants ignore formatting rules – either because they haven't bothered to read them, or because they think their story is so wonderful that the judges will make an exception – and those pieces get weeded out immediately, unread.

Be especially careful about the email heading. If the rules require you to put *'Entry: Udduddu Writing Contest 2021'* then this is exactly what you have to write. The contest organiser's system is programmed to deliver only emails with this precise heading into the folder for the competition. If your email is headed 'My Competition Story' it won't arrive. Even a small mistake – such as a typo, or 'Writer's Contest' instead of 'Writing Contest' means your entry will be lost.

5. FOCUS ON THE THEME, DON'T
JUST MENTION IT

If the contest has a theme – such as 'Mother's Day' or 'Dangerous Insects' – make the theme central to your tale. To win, your story must do more than include the theme – it must be about the theme. For a 'Mother's Day'-themed writing contest, it's not enough that the events happen to play out on Mother's Day. The judges will select an entry that explores the meaning of Mother's Day, with a conflict built around it.

Many entrants, instead of crafting a new story that's perfect for the competition, simply send in an already-written piece, and insert a few words to mention the theme. Years ago, I was on the judging panel for a contest with the theme 'Garden Shed' – and obviously, we were looking for stories which were about garden sheds. But in most entries, a garden shed didn't even play a significant role. The authors merely inserted the words somewhere ('He walked past the garage and the garden shed and rang the doorbell'), expecting to get away with this. Their stories technically qualified – but they were not chosen for the shortlist.

6. INTERPRET THE THEME IN AN UNUSUAL WAY

The contest's theme immediately brings up certain associations. The first idea coming to your mind may be the same that everyone else is thinking of. If you write that story, chances are the judges have already read many similar ones, so yours merely elicits a yawn.

For example, when I helped judge that 'Garden Shed' competition, I got one story after another featuring a husband who spent time in the shed to get away from his wife. I groaned, "Not another one of those." Very few of them made it to the shortlist. I discussed this with the other judges, and they weren't enthusiastic either about reading endless variations of the same story. (One observed that even the names were often the same – husband Albert sought the peace of the garden shed to escape his demanding wife Sally.)

Interpretations that stood out and made it to the shortlist included a man trying to erect an 'easy self-assembly' flat-pack shed, and a woman who coveted a shed so much that she would go to any lengths to obtain it.

7. CHOOSE AN UNEXPECTED POINT OF VIEW

You can make your story stand out by telling it from an unexpected perspective. For example, if the contest theme is 'Wedding', most entries will tell a story in which the main character is the bride. Some others may focus on the groom, a bridesmaid, or the mother of the bride. Take a step away from the obvious and consider who else could be involved in a wedding. How about a caterer, a photographer, or the cleaner dealing with the mess after the event? What might their goals, experiences, dilemmas be?

8. EMPHASISE THE STORY GOAL

What does the main character want or need to achieve during the story, and why? Find a way to state this clearly in the first paragraph, because that's a powerful way to hook readers (including short story judges) and keep them hooked to the end.

At the end, show whether the character has achieved the goal. This will make the ending feel satisfactory to the reader.

In my experience as a short story competition judge, the main weakness of many contest entries is the lack of goal and motivation. Stories in which the main character doesn't need anything, or has no convincing reason for this desire, rarely make it to the shortlist, however beautiful the prose.

9. BEWARE THE ANTICLIMAX

Many contest stories have held my attention with a captivating story goal, well-written prose and a suspenseful plot... and then the ending was a let-down.

The end of the story needs to satisfy the reader by showing whether or not the main character has achieved their goal. The answer can be 'yes' (happy ending) or 'no' (unhappy ending). It can even be 'yes, but' (moderately happy) or 'no, but' (moderately unhappy). But it has to be clear, or the readers (including the contest judges) will feel frustrated.

Most story competition judges have the same pet peeve: stories which end with '... and then the character woke up, because it was only a dream.' Or a simulation or a computer game. These endings are anticlimactic, because they build the reader's suspense, and then deliver nothing at all.

Your story's ending should be more exciting than what came before, giving the readers even more than they expected. Never give the readers less than they anticipate.

10. MAKE SURE YOUR ENTRY FEE ARRIVES

Many contests charge a fee per submission. This is to defray their costs, to make a profit, or to raise funds for a charity. If you don't want to pay the fee, don't enter the contest.

Some writers say, "I don't want to waste my money if my story doesn't win. I'll wait, and if it gets selected, I'll send the payment." But those stories never enter the judging system.

Many contests have automated systems, where you submit electronically and get directed to a payment site. Others expect you to pay by bank transfer or to send a cheque, and with those, the payment can become separated from the entry. I've been involved in several contests where the organisers didn't receive or couldn't find the fees for some entries. The main cause of confusion is that the name of the bank account differs from the name of the email or the pen name on the manuscript.

Make sure it's clear which story the payment is for.

NOVICE MISTAKE TO AVOID

Don't enter a story from the Point-of-View of a dog. Almost every contest I've judged had one or several entries with canine PoV. It seldom works well enough for the story to stand out.

PROFESSIONAL TIP

The best way to make a contest entry stand out is to write something only you can write. Do you live in the Swiss Alps or at the edge of a Yorkshire moor? Then set your tale there, and make the setting an important part of the tale. The place where you live may feel humdrum to you – but to the readers (and the competition judges) it is exciting.

Are you working as garbage collector or a hotel chambermaid? Are you volunteering at an animal rescue shelter, a passionate sailor or devoted to helping the homeless? Then think of a way to interpret the theme in a story about collecting garbage, cleaning hotel rooms, caring for rescued animals, sailing or homelessness.

Your story will have a certain something that other entries don't, and it will ooze realism and authenticity.

ASSIGNMENT

Find contest listings online. (Search for 'short story contests', 'writing competitions' and similar combinations.)

Which of them are a good match for the kind of stories you have written or want to write? Consider your completed stories and unfinished drafts. Could you adapt one of them to match the criteria? If not, identify items from your ideas lists which you could develop into a story to enter into a competition.

THIRTEEN KUKERI

By Rayne Hall

Ching-gronk ching-cronk. The bells on Bogomil's belt clanked with every move. Above their din, he could hear almost nothing, and the eye-holes of his hooded mask restricted his view. With the weight of animal furs and cow bells, his steps lumbered as slow heavy thuds.

Tonight was the night. The Kukeri, resplendent in their grotesque crimson-and-black costumes, were out to clear every home in the village of the demons who resided there.

Bogomil stomped through the next entrance and a low-ceilinged living room. A wood stove with saucepans and couches along the wall indicated that family members lived, cooked and slept in this room. "Eeearrrrhoooo!" he shouted, waved his arms, shambled into the spin.

His comrades Todor and Ivan made a similar racket, filling the small house with their clanks and thuds. The grotesque masks of the Kukeri men were to scare the demons out of hiding and out of the homes. In practice, they scared children, who took cover under beds and behind cupboard doors.

Ah, there was the brat that had used a slingshot against Bogomil's dog, and the girl who had mocked his aged mum. At the memory, heat flushed through his body, and his pulse pounded. Those brats deserved a fright! "Greeeeorghooooo" he roared, and the children screeched, cowering in terror.

How often had he told them to mend their ways, but they ignored his rage, secure in the knowledge that their parents would take their sides. Just thinking of it filled his stomach with sour, roiling resentment. But now he could teach them fear.

He doubted that demons – if they existed – would really take fright at the sight and sound of their human imitators. But the children could be scared.

He made as if to snatch them with his big, shaggy-fur arms, brought his black horned mask right into their faces. Their squeals afforded him pleasant, mild satisfaction.

On his way out, he stopped by the door where the grandmother of the family proffered a tray with dried apricots and rakia. He lifted the fringed flap at his mouth and savoured the sweet chewy fruit. The rakia seared welcome heat down his throat.

Down the front steps, back into the street, spinning in the pale orange light of the street lamps, crunching the newly fallen snow under heavy feet. Watchers stood around along the roadside, hugging their arms close to their chests against the freezing cold. Mittened children sat on their fathers' shoulders, some waving, but screaming when the demon-men came close.

Inside his animal fur costume, with the hooded mask covering is face, Bogomil sweated.

Clank clank clank. The Kukeri men danced down the road, the copper cowbells on their harnesses chinking and clonking.

He noted with satisfied approval that the members of the team had beautified and embellished their costumes, as he had encouraged them to. They had kept the characteristic crimson cone-shaped mask hoods of their village forefathers but added creative touches. Now the masks, adorned with beads, sequins and mirrors to reflect the ugly face of evil, featured sculpted noses and mouths studded with pointed teeth. Fantastical shapes framed the heads with deer antlers, cow horns and turkey feathers. They looked grotesque, terrifying and mesmerising: true demons. He waved to signal which dancers were to enter which house next.

He counted the men as they hopped between the frozen puddles on the snow-blanketed dirt road: twelve dancers, including himself. Everyone had turned up. Excellent. The choreography would unfold as rehearsed. In previous years, the village Kukeri had not rehearsed, simply donned their costumes and shuffled randomly around, their bells sounding like a herd of stampeding cows.

But Bogomil had bigger plans. He envisioned an impressive performance, and he needed twelve rehearsed dancers for that. A smaller group wouldn't look impressive in the square, and some of the formations he'd drilled them in wouldn't work. Now he could put his worries to rest. His persuasion and organisation skills had paid off. He jumped in triumph. "Eeeerrrah!"

Another house, another round of scaring demons into leaving. No rakia this time, but a banknote. He was pleased. He'd persuaded the troupe members that all gifts of money should go towards repairing the memorial fountain, something the current mayor claimed the village had no funds for.

Now, towards the village square, past the old walnut trees with their gnarled winter-bare branches, past the schoolhouse with the barred windows, past the pretty church. Dogs strained their chains, barking and yowling as the big noisy creatures marched by.

The villagers would be stunned to see a real show, with choreography and rhythm. Word must have spread about the rehearsals and that there was going to be a real spectacle tonight.

Drummers and a bagpiper led the procession, followed by the village women in their traditional embroidered dresses, their scarlet headscarves crowned with wreaths of pink plastic blooms. Black quilted jackets marred the picturesque effect.

On the Eastern horizon, the first ink-blue of dawn was rising into the black of the night. Bogomil had timed it perfectly. They would finish their display minutes before sunrise, because the sun must never catch a Kukeri on the road.

Now they reached the square with the monument to Bulgaria's liberation next to the night-shuttered grocery store, and the mayoral office with its big portal, flanked by the Bulgarian and European flags.

The women stepped aside and the drummers took up their spots and drummed the rhythm – *ratat ratatatat* as the Kukeri demons spilled their power into the square, their fur-clad movements still a disjointed jingle of bells, with their Bogomil leading from the front.

The bagpipe whined its repetitive tune, then fell silent, while the drums grew louder, more dramatic. *Ratat ratatatat.*

Now. Bogomil switched to the rhythmic stride, and the others fell in behind him. Then the hops, the full body sways. The cow bells created their own rhythm, loud and fierce, relegating the drums to mere background whispers.

A torch bearer, muffled against the cold in a thick cap and shawl, lit the central fire, a narrow pyramid of sticks flaming fast and orange into the sky.

At Bogomil's sign, the Kukeri formed a circle, each man spinning around himself, a structured formation, yet untamed, wild.

Under their steps, the white fluffy snow darkened, then turned to slush.

Ah, there was his wife, standing on the steps leading to the mayor's office, beneath the white-green-red Bulgarian flag, filming with her new smartphone. He raised his hand, smiling, although Katya wouldn't be able to see his face. She understood the greeting, raised her hand in response, without lowering the camera. He could see she was pleased with the turnout and proud of what he had achieved.

He'd use this video to publicise the village once he was mayor, part of his strategy to gain renown and attract visitors.

The men hopped and whirled in unison, and every move sent the shaggy hairs of their fur suits flying and the bells donging and clinking their message: demons begone!

Bogomil was proud of his team and satisfied with his achievement. All through the year he had watched videos of Bulgarian folk dances, had studied the male dancers' displays. He had adapted their steps and formations, combining authenticity with innovation, tradition with audience-rousing visual appeal. Of course, the heavy costumes precluded intricate footwork and high leaps, but he had incorporated the group formations with fluid transitions between spirals, grapevines, domino effects and weaves. The highlight would be a formation of his own devising he called the Thracian wheel, which was sure to make jaws drop.

Already the villagers, standing along the square's edge, hands in pockets for warmth, stared and whistled in appreciation.

Bogomil's thoughts, his work, all had paid off. When the time came for the mayoral election, the villagers would remember the man who had organised the spectacular display. "If he can handle the Kukeri, he can handle the gypsies, the road sweepers, the snow clearance, the bureaucrats," they would say.

The Kukeri melded into quartets, pairs, triplets, pairs again.... Wait. Bogomil's chest tightened. Something was wrong.

One of the dancers had joined the wrong group. Four dancers rotated in what should be a triplet behind the fire pyramid. Never mind. The men did as he had instructed: when one made a mistake, just keep moving, as if you had intended to do this all along. The errant performer would resume his correct place in the next formation.

But now… another mistake. This was the figure of three quartets, and suddenly there were five in his own circle. Which group lacked a dancer? He'd better steer towards them, so the man who'd lost his place could switch smoothly.

But the other circles had the correct number of four dancers each.

Sweat trickled down his temples inside the woollen mask. Was there a dancer too many?

He counted. One, two, three…. Eleven, twelve. And himself: thirteen.

Impossible. They were twelve. Had the rakia affected his brain?

He counted once more. No mistake: There were thirteen Kukeri where they should be twelve. What was going on?

His mind raced through possibilities. Someone must have joined spontaneously, perhaps one of the old men who used to run with the Kukeri in previous years, unaware that this year they had rehearsed a choreography.

Yes, this must be it. One of the seniors who had declared themselves too old to participate, moaning about the weight of the bell harness pressing down on arthritic knees, hadn't been able to resist the itch to join the Kukeri one more time. Hopefully, the interloper would soon realise that he was out of his depth and withdraw.

But… now the dancers were breaking into two lines, the way they had rehearsed. All thirteen of them. How could an interloper know what to do?

It had to be old Stoyan who had actually come to the first rehearsals, but grumbled about having to learn a choreography and resigned, leaving Bogomil to find a replacement fast. Obviously, Stoyan must have changed his mind – but why hadn't he let Bogomil and the others know? And how could someone who had only grudgingly joined a couple of walk-throughs blend so smoothly with the well-rehearsed troupe?

One line was shorter than the other, but each performed the series of hops he had devised for this stage: right-left-right, left-right-left, forward-back-forward, right spin….The display was smooth, without a glitch.

Now, pairs, with each hooking a thumb into his partner's belt. Bogomil found himself partnered not with one, but two men. Two hands hooked into his belt, and while he was almost frozen to the spot, they dragged him into their spin.

One of them was Ivan in his rightful place. The other was…. Who? And which of them was Ivan, the one he could trust? He thought he recognised the mask with the sequins arranged to look like the face of a skull… but the second dancer had adapted a similar design, and both wore elaborate structures with feathers and horns around their heads. Ivan had promised to embellish his costume for the show but had not revealed details.

Bogomil's head spun. He wished he hadn't drunk the rakia.

A new formation. Fours, threes…. Hot sweat ran down his sides. He counted, counted again. Twelve dancers, plus himself. That made thirteen.

If he could identify the interloper, he could evict him, of course pretending that it was part of the rehearsed display. But which one?

The dancer with the black calf-wraps tied in white ribbons was out of synch. No – that was young Mikhail, who always started the grapevine on the wrong foot.

Bogomil felt, rather than saw, the others look at him through their masks. Twelve beaded, sequinned faces were turned to him. They wanted him, their leader, to provide an explanation.

He wished he could smile reassurance at them, but the masks prevented facial communication. So he just danced on.

Perhaps someone who begrudged Bogomil's efficiency and success had decided to sabotage the event. Had a rival with mayoral aspirations spied on the group's rehearsals to throw the formations into disarray?

Whoever he was, so far he was fitting in. As long as the interloper got the steps right and moved in the right direction, the show could go on. The performance would work with thirteen as well as it worked with twelve.

Then it hit him with cold force. The Thracian Wheel! The complex highlight of the performance – it needed precisely twelve dancers to work. He knew this, because he had tried to adapt it to ten and eleven when men had skipped the rehearsals. The result had been an embarrassing mess.

Could he himself simply step aside, and let the other twelve perform? But no. He was needed as the linchpin who understood the pattern and whose hands could guide each dancer to their specific place. The Thracian Wheel wasn't something where the participants could just go with the flow and improvise.

In organising the performance, he had made contingency plans for every eventuality, including a dancer not turning up on the night. If the troupe was a dancer short, the Thracian Wheel had to be cut.

The showpiece. The formation that would look spectacular on video, bring attention to the village and its traditions, cement his reputation as a man who could organise a horde of mummers into an accomplished act.

He made a decision. As they went into the Brotherly Circle, each with his arms around his neighbour's shoulder, he said to the man on his right, *"Leave out the Thracian Wheel. Pass the word. No*

Thracian Wheel. Go straight into side hops." He had to shout above the din. He saw the word being passed.

Then he said the same to his neighbour on the left, in case the intruder wasn't passing it on.

Word passed. He saw quick flicks of the head, denoting 'yes' as each dancer was informed. And so that's what they did.

In the centre, the flames leaped higher, as if fanned by this sacrifice. They shone their orange light on the dark heaps of slush and glistened on the wet flagstones.

The men went into side hops. The glorious performance didn't happen, but they didn't embarrass themselves either. The performance was grotesque, terrifying, wild – like the demons they were dancing to expel.

Understanding slammed into Bogomil's stomach, hard and cold as a lump of ice. Demons.

No human could perform the dance without learning it first.

Instead of expelling the demons from the village houses, they had invited one of them to join.

They?

He, Bogomil had. As a Kukeri, he was supposed to drive out negativity, and instead, he had thought with anger, resentment and malice about children.

Now that demon was mocking him.

Then the horizon brightened with strips of morning pink, and he spun into the centre, the sign for everyone else to break up.

The Kukeri clanked off the square, and the village women lined up for their folk dance in the first rays of the morning sun.

The village restaurant's doors opened in warm welcome. The Kukeri crowded into the low-ceilinged room. On the stone wall between icons of St George and St Michael hung photos of Kukeri troupes from decades ago. Yellow flames prattled in the fireplace. On the wooden tables waited flasks of hot coffee and trays with rakia.

Now the intruder would be exposed. Bogomil watched narrowly as hood after hood came off.

The fantastic heads with their feathers and antlers were detached from the shaggy bodies, set on tables where they looked lifeless but still grotesque. Faces emerged…. And every one of them a member of the team.

As the men unstrapped the heavy bell harnesses, stepped out of the hairy trousers, unwound the wrappings around their calves, Bogomil counted.

Eleven men. Plus himself. That made twelve – the number they should have been.

He said, "Well done, this was really great," the way he had planned to praise them. But the words came out in a croak, and he didn't continue.

There was none of the triumphant cheer that should conclude a successful performance, none of the backslapping and jokes. Instead, the men ran their hands across their foreheads and through the hair, fumbled to adjust their everyday clothing. Todor covertly made the sign of the cross.

Bogomil cleared his throat. "There was a thirteenth dancer. Who? And where is he now?"

Ivan reached for a rakia-filled glass and emptied it in one gulp. "Maybe we've been mistaken."

The others tilted their heads in hopeful acknowledgement of the possibility, willing to believe anything but what they had seen with their own eyes.

"It'll be on video," Mikhail said, gazing at the St George icon on the stone wall. "Your wife has filmed everything, hasn't she? Let's look at the video, then we can see how many there were. Shall I ask her to give me her camera now?"

Everyone was in agreement, as if seeing the video would confirm that the thirteenth was only an illusion.

But Bogomil didn't want to watch the video. He knew what it would show: the twelve dancers of his troop, and with them, the demon.

GUNDA'S GNOMES

By Rayne Hall

Daffodils nodded their golden heads, tulips stood in waxy splendour, and early hyacinths spread their heady scent across the allotment garden. Savouring the rare sunshine and silence, Gunda polished her gnomes with a soft cloth until each red cap shone.

She knew the name of every one, from the conventional store-bought ones who carried watering cans and leaned on spades, to the special editions which could be found only in her garden. She wiped a pigeon dropping off Arabella's sleek shoulder, straightened the drooping Anthony, and placed Angling Ajax next to the water butt.

The robin in the hawthorn screeched a warning, and her new allotment neighbour marched down the garden path, shoulders wide, elbows to the side, designer wellies crunching twigs underfoot. "Playing with your toys again, Gunda?" His chuckle dripped with oily contempt. "A lady of your advanced years?"

He clanked his portable stereo on the bench and flipped it into grating life. A male voice panted over throbbing metallic rhythms, shattering the peace.

He smoothed his creased trousers and barked orders into his mobile phone. "No later than Thursday! That's your job! Get it done!" Then he peered at Gunda through purple-tinted glasses.

Crouching by the daffodil border, she tried to ignore him, but her stomach fermented with anger and her heart started to pound.

"Aren't you ashamed playing with dolly-gnomes still?"

With trembling fingers, Gunda kept polishing a special edition gnome who carried a briefcase and wore an old school tie.

"Are you deaf, or what? I asked you a question!" His wellingtons trod across her freshly dug vegetable bed, crushing the soil into clods, and stopped barely a finger-breath from her knees. "Answer me. Are you ashamed?"

"I like my gnomes," Gunda defended without lifting her gaze. Her voice sounded feeble even to her own ears. "And most allotment plot holders admire them."

He sneered and kicked at a gnome, toppling it over. Gunda yelped.

He laughed, and kicked another one. And another, and another. They skittered across the beds. One landed on a paving slab with a harsh chink.

Gunda ran to inspect the damage. "Her nose is chipped!"

"Are you going to cry?"

She pressed the wounded gnome to her chest.

He marched close up to her. "Are you?"

"I'll complain to the allotment committee about this." She meant to say this with calm and dignity, but it came out as a desperate squeak. She had already appealed to the new committee to restrain this new plotholder's behaviour, but they had shrugged off her pleas. They did not like trouble; they had no cause to believe her; without witnesses, it was her word against his.

His laughter sounded like a big dog's bark. "Get a life, woman! It's only a gnome."

He strode back to his own plot, where he turned the stereo volume up higher and popped a can of lager.

Gunda ran a tender finger across the little figure in her hands. The vandalised victim was not one of the special edition gnomes, but precious nevertheless, and the injured face would not heal. She straightened and spoke with slow determination. "I expect you to pay for the damage."

"Expect all you want, woman. But you can't prove a thing." He ripped couch-grass from his cabbage bed and flicked it into Gunda's garden. "Prove that, too."

Only the flaming fury in her guts kept the tears from streaming down her face. She knew his type, of course. A coward and weakling, he made himself feel big by bullying others. She was his chosen victim simply because there was something different about her. Where others grew peas and potatoes, she cultivated gnomes.

It was the story of her life. Unpleasant people always homed in on her like slugs on a cabbage leaf. Even as a child she'd been bullied because her mum made her wear hand-knit sweaters instead of shop-bought ones. In her teens, her studiousness had singled her out, and in her twenties, it was her ambition at work.

Shutting out the provocations, she focused on polishing her gnomes. But when he tossed the empty beer can into her little pond, anger spiralled from the bottom of her belly up into her throat. She wanted to yell at the bully, but of course that never solved anything.

She remembered what her college counsellor had suggested for whenever she felt angry or helpless: imagine the tormentors as oinking piglets or knee-high gnomes.

The piglets idea had been fun, but gnomes had worked better for Gunda. Over the years she had refined the method on the jerks who made her life miserable. The snotty bank manager who refused her a loan, the landlady snooping in her drawers, the neighbour whose rap recordings pounded until long after midnight, the boss who always pinched her bottom – whenever she transformed them mentally into garden gnomes, she felt better.

Indeed, this was what had inspired her interest in collecting gnomes.

The allotment bully was coming again, with his designer-booted swagger heavy with importance, beer can in one hand, a bunch of chopped brambles in the other. He planted himself on the boundary path between their plots, pushing his toes into her seed bed. Slowly, he crunched the can in his fist. It popped and whooshed with hollow sounds of metallic pain. He flicked it at Gunda's feet. Then he scattered thorny bramble pieces over Gunda's freshly-raked seedbed.

If she hurried to pick up his droppings, he would savour her submission. If she left them even for a short time, the brambles pieces would dig themselves into the soil, and if she missed even one, her garden would be infested with thorny bramble weeds for years.

With clenched teeth, she fought for self-control, and lost. The heat in her stomach had reached boiling point. It was time to apply the anger management technique.

She tightened the roaring anger that spiralled through her body into tight coils. Blood throbbed through her limbs, and her skin tingled all over. In her mind, she painted a picture of him at a tenth of his size, with a pointy red hat that went well with the designer wellies. Then she focused and released her balled fury.

When the energy hit him, he gasped. "Saint Mercury!" Then there was a whining sound, like air whistling out of a pierced balloon.

Gunda watched with glee. The morphing moments were always so satisfying.

Right before her eyes, the bully shrank. He opened his mouth to scream, but no sound came. His expression was frozen in wide-eyed horror.

Exhausted from the effort, but satisfied with the result, Gunda waited until the calf-high figure solidified and was cool to the touch.

Then she placed it by the compost heap, between the bank manager and the bottom-pinching boss.

DEAR READER,

I hope you found these tips helpful, that you have created a story you're proud of, and are brimming with ideas for more enchanting tales.

You could really help me by writing a review about this book and posting it on a bookselling website, or perhaps in an online book-reading group, your social media or your blog. Maybe you can mention the kind of fiction you write (or plan to write), and explain which chapters you found most helpful and why.

Email me the link to your review, and I'll send you a free review copy (ebook) of one of my other Writer's Craft books. Let me know which one you would like. There are around 40 to choose from, so you can pick the one which will be most helpful at this stage of your journey as a writer. (For a title list with brief descriptions, see this page on my website www.raynehall.com/books-for-writers).

My email is contact@raynehall.com. Drop me a line if you've spotted any typos which have escaped the proof-reader's eagle eyes, or want to give me private feedback or have questions.

You can also contact me on Twitter: https://twitter.com/RayneHall. Tweet me that you've read this book, and I'll probably follow you back.

If you want to hear from me more often, I have a newsletter with writing tips, mini writing contests, special offers, information about upcoming books, and glimpses into my life in Bulgaria and adventures with my rescue cats. To subscribe, go to my website. On the home page https://www.raynehall.com, scroll down and you'll see the subscribe link to the newsletter. Subscribers get a free pdf ebook, *Grow Your Author Voice.*

If you find this book helpful, it would be great if you could spread the word about it. Maybe you know other writers who would benefit.

With best wishes for your writing success, and hopes to see your stories published in great anthologies,

Rayne Hall

ACKNOWLEDGEMENTS

I give sincere thanks to writers who read the draft chapters and offered valuable feedback: Jules Ironside, Cage Dunn, Ann Maguire.

The book cover is by Erica Syverson and Jasmine Bailey. Julia Gibbs proofread the manuscript, and Eled Cernik formatted the book.

And finally, I say thank you to my sweet cats Sulu and Uhura who took turns snuggling on the desk between my arms while I typed.

Rayne Hall

BOOKS IN THE WRITER'S CRAFT SERIES

You can read them in any order. Which of them would be most helpful for your current writing project?

Writing Fight Scenes

Writing Scary Scenes

The Word-Loss Diet

Writing About Magic

Writing About Villains

Writing Dark Stories

Euphonics For Writers

Writing Short Stories to Promote Your Novels

Twitter for Writers

Why Does My Book Not Sell? 20 Simple Fixes, Writing Vivid Settings

How To Train Your Cat To Promote Your Book

Writing Deep Point of View

Getting Book Reviews

Novel Revision Prompts

Writing Vivid Dialogue

Writing Vivid Characters

Writing Book Blurbs and Synopses

Writing Vivid Plots

Write Your Way Out Of Depression: Practical Self-Therapy For Creative Writers

Fantasy Writing Prompts

Horror Writing Prompts

How to Write That Scene

More Horror Writing Prompts

Writing Love Scenes

Author Branding

Fiction Pacing

Ghostwriting

Writing Gothic Fiction

Fiction Pacing

Copywriting

Writing Romance Novels and Love Stories

Writing and Publishing a Book Series

Writing and Publishing Short Stories

… and more

Printed in Dunstable, United Kingdom